BOOK ONE

FEARLESS

Ending Your Unconsciousness

ANDREW HACKETT

HOLLAND HOUSE
PUBLISHING

NEW YORK

ENDING YOUR UNCONCIOUSNESS
Copyright ©2018 Andrew Hackett

All rights reserved. No part of this book may be used or reproduced in any manner whatsoever without written permission except in the case of brief quotations embodied in critical articles or reviews.

For information contact:
HollandHousePublishing.com

ISBN: 978-0-578-41809-4
First Edition: November 2018

10 9 8 7 6 5 4 3 2 1

I want to dedicate this series, as I do
my everyday, to my Hero.

The Hero that has made everything possible.
My Hero is also my greatest teacher, a beautiful soul,
unashamebly human in every way.

This Hero is You.

You are the Hero of this story
and in turn you are my greatest Hero. I dedicate
everything I know to your greatest achievement, although
it has not yet happened, I know for certain, it will.

Because together, we will make sure it does.

CONTENTS

Preface 13

Introduction: Let the Journey Begin 27

1. My Truth Does Not Have to Be Your Truth 35

2. Why Do Some Teacher's Words Resonate? 43

3. Love and Fear 53

4. We Create Our Own Life Experience 61

5. Your Ego 69

6. The Universe is A Mirror 77

7. Judgment is Not Working For You 85

8. Forgive Yourself and Set Yourself Free 93

9. Fear is An Illusion 101

10. We Always Have a Choice 119

11. Your Beliefs and Why You Need to Change Them 129

12. Your Uniqueness Will Lead You to Your Life Purpose 141

13. From Unconscious to Awakening 151

About the Author 159

DISCLAIMER: This book provides the personal experiences and beliefs of the author. It is sold with the understanding that neither the author nor the publisher is engaged in rendering legal, accounting, medical, psychological, or other professional services. If legal or other professional advice is warranted, the services of an appropriate professional should be sought. Neither author nor publisher accepts any liability or responsibility to any person or entity with respect to any loss or damage alleged to have been caused, directly or indirectly, by the information, ideas, opinions or other content in this book. If you do not agree to these terms, you should immediately return this book for a full refund.

(Above based on a jointly-adopted declaration by American Publishers Association and American Bar Association.)

Preface

I sit quietly by the water, watching the dragonflies skim the water in search of sustenance and nourishment. They operate in a different time and space continuum, like the hummingbird. A dragonfly pauses in front of me, as if looking into my soul. It must find humans like me fascinating. Fascinating like only a highly-evolved creature can look upon the unconscious. Their speed, agility and grace are in stark comparison to my slow, bulky caveman appearance, like a Neanderthal stumbling around in the dark - hungry and unknowing.

The dragonfly reaches into my mind, only to find nothing of any real substance. Pure in its purpose, knowing why it is here on this beautiful, mother-loved planet. I wonder, is this what highly-evolved beings think? Do they reach into our minds only to see

ENDING YOUR UNCONSCIOUSNESS

emptiness, confusion and the ego-driven fog that consumes us all? I'm not talking about arrogant, egoic idiots, puffing their chests out and throwing their weight around hoping to intimidate (although that is part of the problem). I'm talking about the Ego that lives within each and every one of us, the voice in our head, like the parrot on our shoulder. The ever-clever Ego, relentlessly pursuing control over its host: Us.

The Ego manifests as both all things and some things, to everyone. For some, it is the chest-puffing idiot; for others, the victim. The bully, the successful, the judgemental and the cruel. The dragonfly is none of these things - without Ego, and without care of the problems of the world. It just is what it is: a dragonfly, going about its business, pausing in curious wonder, as to what this lump is before it, staring back at it, wondering, searching for connection.

The dragonfly abruptly moves on, without the awkward goodbyes that humans inanely seem to love so much. The sun is unusually warm on this late winter's day, bouncing off the rhythmical pulses of the gentle ocean - calm, quiet, lapping at the sands of this day's mystery. As I sit and wonder what's next for me, my mind wanders to years past, to the journey I have been on. I have enjoyed every step, albeit not knowing it at the time. The Universe has brought me great wonder, and great lessons,

PREFACE

until my next... challenge? Opportunity? What is this I now seek? Little do I know the Universe already knows the answer. I don't have the right answers because I have yet to ask the right questions.

One thing I know about the Universe is that it is merely here to respond. To respond to our curiosities, our questions and to our desires. It is a miracle of complexity and intelligence that can organise, conspire, influence and create like no other, but it is as much a part of us as we are a participant in its magnificent glory. Years of personal ingression into the depths of my psychology has enabled me to grasp the reality that the Universe is non-judgemental, completely unbiased towards our thoughts, feelings or choices, insomuch as to realise that the creation of my life to date has been completely of my own creative being.

Everything that has culminated as my life experience has occurred as a result of my own being rather than any divinely-instructed purpose on behalf of some Deity. This is not to say we don't have a role to play, and that role is divine as is any other; but more to say that the Universe doesn't dictate what must happen, but only responds to the choices we make of what we desire our life to be.

As the water laps, the occasional fish (whose desire to fly like a bird is short-lived with the introduction of gravity) distracts me

ENDING YOUR UNCONSCIOUSNESS

from my quiet reflection - a beautiful soul that I have noticed a couple times in the last few minutes, shuffling awkwardly in the sand, has made me wonder. I see your energy, not as a sight, but as a knowing - a troubled past of confusion fuelled by the desire to understand. It is a sight, not of form, but of understanding, of compassionate hearing; not of words, but of emotional communication. As you draw closer I see a panicky courage rise within you as you approach me with a new-found purpose. What could this be, I wonder?

I see you now, within the pages your eyes are cast upon. Seeking a truth that has been sparked by your once dormant curiosity. You have had this curiosity awakened by the words of a simple man of everyday breeding. Your search for the truth, to be set free from the complexities of your fear-driven mind, has brought you here: to the cool sand, to the warm sun, as you reluctantly and unexpectedly stand before me. I see the sun on your face, its reflection in your eyes, as they shift to prevent my observation of what is happening within you. You guardedly excuse your interruption of my quiet self-reflection, as your search for the words, that cause your stomach to churn and your feet to shuffle uncontrollably, accelerates rapidly.

"Hi. How are you?" I say, seeking to reassure you that I am happy to connect with you, to converse (albeit it in the shallows

PREFACE

for now). "Are you O.K.?" I ask. You interrupt with the relief of having spoken, almost for the first time it seems. You have been thinking of this moment for a while, not for celebrity or fandom, but for an inner need to reach out. You quickly realise that I am approachable and friendly, and I invite you to sit and stare at the quiet ocean with me so we both may feel the afternoon's warm winter sun on our back. You gratefully accept and find a comfortable position in the cool sand. As your breathing settles you find yourself becoming comfortable next to me.

We sit briefly in silence, as the soul often does as it searches for the meaning in a good book they cannot put down. I feel your energy relax, until you notice you are sitting awkwardly close, our elbows touching, bottoms firmly held by the cool sand. I reach out with my hand to firmly grasp your shaking elbow, and reassure you with a gentle touch, that this is O.K., even for strangers that haven't met. You pause, wondering how I am hearing your inner dialogue, how am I seeing what you have not yet shown. This channel of thought takes over as your curiosity rises within you, until you realise that you are relaxed, feeling at peace with what is happening. No longer feeling guilty for your interruption as you learn to know that I am completely O.K. with it. I am at peace, with a peace that starts to wash over you. Although you haven't felt like this for many a year, you are

ENDING YOUR UNCONSCIOUSNESS

excited for its warm arrival, embracing it with every bit of your soul. You feel like you have arrived home after a long period away.

You start to explain, with hushed tones (almost as though we were surrounded by people and they somehow care to know what we are about to explore) that you have deliberately sought me out to ask me questions - and so many have been arising within you. Your thoughts about this moment have been long coming when they once started within the exploration of my first book. You don't believe in the modern way - searching online, watching from the shadows, curious, wanting to reach out and connect with someone, believing the connection to not be quite real. So, you sought to find me and to sit, old-fashioned like, in each other's energy, so that you could feel the energy of my responses. Almost as if to bask in the connection between two divine souls, like we bask in the warm winter's sunlight.

This is all very new to you and you are unconscious to what your soul desires. You have little understanding – really none at all, until recently, when you first moved your wide eyes over my words. Your world has opened up to new possibilities and given you a new courage, if only to ask the right questions to the right person. I enjoy feeling your energy relax into the moment as I sit attentively, remaining present with your enquiry. You open up

PREFACE

your heart and spill your life onto the sand before me, and we both embark on a dark journey of long-lost impulsive decisions and unrequited dreams being replaced with controlled choices, manufactured desires and a life experienced through the wishes of how others see how the world should be.

You talk at length about the unhappiness that has risen within you, not one of sadness per se, but of an unlived life, a missed purpose and a knowing that life is running out. You seek (like I seek) to be the change you wish to see in the world. You desire (like I desire) to arrive at your death bed knowing you did everything you possibly could - once you knew you were, in fact, capable. Sometimes you find yourself gushing over the opening of your heart to the words you hear from me and pull back as though to not look foolish. Although my Ego rises in hearing such words, I gently and lovingly set it aside to maintain the presence with you, that I also seek from you.

As time passes, the sun moves slowly lower into the sky and we both notice the chill of the winter's evening start to roll in across the water. I see your discomfort rise from the cold, but your determination to continue is strong, as you have waited too long for this moment. Now that you have finally accepted that I am O.K. with you and your beautiful playful energy, I suggest we find a warmer place inside, where the smell of food is hot and

ENDING YOUR UNCONSCIOUSNESS

hearty, and we can explore this obviously synchronistic event some more. It is clear we are now friends, for you have settled into my company, without fear or anticipation. I now understand the moment, both for what it is, and for what will become of it. It is clear to me now. The synchronicity is obvious.

Much time has passed since my first book, written years before this moment now, and much has come to pass to be recognised for what it is. My life is settled, solid and abundant, and not for a change in monetary wealth, but for the wealth that has come from helping those that seek real, unqualified change in their life. I have learnt that success is not a figure, but a moment in the journey of the peaceful at heart. It is not the Ferrari nor the luxury waterfront home, but the moments like this - universally synchronistic in every way.

You have found me out of my way, in another place and time, as it turns out by happenstance. You recognised me earlier in the day, wandering this fine town, in search for adventure, and thought it was reasonable to approach. You were right, as I know the benefit of allowing and surrendering to the moment. It is important to me to do so, because it enables me to put aside my protective, controlling, fear-constructed measures.

We sit, talking freely into the darkening evening, ordering a meal and keeping warm by the fire. As the room fills with more

PREFACE

and more people seeking a range of connections and disconnections alike, it fails to bother you, as you slowly unpack your life before me. Your energy is softer now: less guarded, more warm and friendly. You are obviously a kind, old soul who in this life believes you have lost your way. I don't think of it so much as that, especially since I know the journey is not really a journey without a place to start. I have worked with many souls and all who have come for answers have done so from the low point in their lives that triggered the need. I see it as a blessing; a rock bottom of sorts, because it is often exactly what we need to enable us to see what needs to be done.

Your questions run into the night. Three courses down and we are full and seeking more comfort. It is clear to me what you seek by now, and also clear what needs to be. Your understanding has come a long way, through the seeking and searching that has come, from the asking of many questions, to books like mine. You have found truth in the words of a few teachers, and we talk readily about what you feel and why.

This rising within you is happening now for a reason. This curiosity is purposeful in the Universe's direction. Synchronicities like this don't happen for any reason; they happen for good reason. You know this already, so I feel no need to explain. You find yourself in a not-so-unique point in your life

ENDING YOUR UNCONSCIOUSNESS

where you are seeking the truth, but you don't know what you don't know. You feel blind sometimes to what it all means, why you are here, and more importantly, what you are supposed to do. Like a superhero with no cause, you sit here with me seeking answers, not from a great teacher, but from someone who merely has been there before. This is all a reflection from the Universe of your soul's desire to awaken. Your desire is strong and constant, unrelenting in its purpose.

I suggest in earnest that a journey has begun for you, as I know that you have already packed your metaphorical bags while you wait for the opportunity to arise. You seek to end the unconsciousness of your existence, to awaken to what desires stir deep within. This is not a sexual thing by any means, as it is a deeper, soul-drawn need for a real existence of meaning and exploration. This is beyond the mere physicality of sexual expression; your heart craves what is knows the soul has access to and you are determined to explore it, like the early explorers of humanity's expansion. You feel like the early explorers, but more like exploring the wastelands of your lost years. You need to sit within your own life's puzzle and find a home for every lost piece. This is a journey that has arisen within you from the moment you decided to follow the path that your soul decided for you. You have forever known, since that very day, that you had

PREFACE

strayed into the wrong track. Now it is up to you, for there is another fork in the road ahead of you. You still see it there now.

It peels onto two very different paths. One is of unconscious living, not knowing the answers to the questions you simply cannot understand enough to ask. That path is full of old friends, from past choices and consequences. Friends that at the time felt good and free, but with the benefit of hindsight, you now know weren't serving you at all.

The other path is a journey of great personal exploration and growth. A path of immense emotional upheaval and a path overseen by the knowledge that you have to relearn everything. You intuitively see down this path that every belief you had once fostered will be challenged in ways you cannot comprehend. You see that friends from the past cannot travel this road with you because they simply don't care enough to do so. You know there are new friends to find, new lovers to enjoy and a new version of yourself to create. This path frightens you as much as it excites you, and for the first time in decades you feel freer than you can ever remember.

My intuition enables this discussion to take place, as we explore the possibilities and the complexities. I see the excitement you hold for your future, as you clearly see it for the first time, with your eyes truly open. I explain that this path isn't for

ENDING YOUR UNCONSCIOUSNESS

everyone, and it takes great resilience, commitment and work, but you feel too alive with so much promise and possibility to care too much about the hard work for now.

Let me grab the bill, and we shall go into the winter's night, for spring is upon us and there is no better time to spend exploring the ways of the Universe than in the season of beginning. But before we get there, there are some things you need to know, and I promise I will be there every step of the way. The journey you are about to embark on is your journey and only you can travel it. I will reside with you, as your rudder through stormy seas. But you must always remember, the sun shines its brightest after the heavy rain, and before we can assemble the new you, first we must disassemble the old you.

Finish your drink and grab your coat. It is cold outside, and the weather has closed in. The wind is howling, the rain sleeting, and the creatures will be damp and cold. This path that we shall undertake needs preparation.

It has been a delightful evening, and I have loved your company so. It is always such a pleasure to sit with a beautiful soul in search of meaning and great possibilities. This is the day you will remember, not as your finest moment (for that is most certainly yet to come) but as the day you made the beginning of your new life - the day that triggered your awakening to who you

PREFACE

truly are.

Come, my friend. Let's get you home to pack - for we need to start early tomorrow; because if we haven't started by tomorrow's noon, you surely will have developed cold feet.

Sleep with the Angels, for they keep you in great company. They are pleased with your choice and they are celebrating tonight, for tomorrow they know you will need their strength. You are never alone on this path, unless you choose to be, but only you can tread upon it. This is by design, the Universe's brilliance. And soon you will know why.

Tomorrow is the ending of your unconsciousness, and the sun will rise, brighter than you will have ever known. The path toward the conscious life is a hard one, but one of unparalleled beauty. The synchronicity of these pages suggests as much, but none as much as your reading of them.

*"We are but beings, lost without compassion.
Ruled by the sonnet of Fear's Chorus.
Easily controlled by unconscious choice, forever
lost until we find the light."*

The Wise Old Man

Introduction: Let the Journey Begin

We all travel a journey that manifests as our life experience. The challenge is that most of us are travelling a path that doesn't match with the expectation of what we thought life would be. This leaves us feeling unsatisfied with the life we are experiencing and leads to unhappiness drawn from a lack of fulfillment, and eventually, depression.

We are told that we just need to suck it up, get on with it, and accept the fact that this is what life is about. The problem is, that is simply a lie told by the uninitiated, the uneducated or the lazy. The truth of the matter is that life is whatever you make it

ENDING YOUR UNCONSCIOUSNESS

out to be. It is your decision, and it always has been. In fact, the life you are currently leading (albeit unsatisfactory) is a creation of you own choices, or lack thereof. Because even the lack of a choice is a choice in its own right.

I lived this lie for decades, and although I did ok, I wasn't happy. Although I was successful in the eyes of some, in my mind I wasn't living up to my potential. I wasn't really living. That is until I realised that life didn't happen *to* me, but *for* me. Until I realised that our destiny is not what we are supposed to *do*, but what we have *become*. Until I realised that everything in my life experience is a culmination of my own choices, beliefs and desires; and if there was ever anything that I could influence or control in my life, that it was my choices, my beliefs or my desires.

What you will find in these pages is a culmination of decades of discovery, analysis, and trial and error. I share this with you in the hope that you will not only find yourself, but also find your path towards the magnificence that you came here to live. I hold a place deep in my heart as I watch over your journey in amazement of everything life has to offer. I long for the connection created within these pages, to be long lasting within you, in the hope that I might help in some small way to enable you to find the truth you have been longing for, for so long.

INTRODUCTION

I write my thoughts for your guidance across five clear stages. These five stages are covered throughout the Fearless Series, to ensure you have every process, every tool and every understanding necessary to become the master of your own destiny. Each book provides a unique perspective and a unique approach to each stage, each of which must be put into action to ensure the best results. It is covered across the five books in as effective and efficient way as possible to make it as easy for you as it can be, despite the fact that explaining every aspect and each and every context in the finest of detail would take decades to write, and even longer to consume.

Remember: what you are embarking on is easily the most difficult thing you will ever set out to accomplish in your life and also the most rewarding. Once you have arrived you will also deem it to have been the easiest journey, because at this point it will all make complete sense. If that is the case, then I will have achieved what I have set out to achieve: that is, to free you from your bondage, set you on your path to realise great achievements, and to do so in as easy a fashion as I know how.

Remember, the destination cannot be reached without the journey, and in reality, the destination is the illusion, as the journey is the only thing that is real. Each step upon the hallowed path is necessary to ensure the right path is taken, for skipping

ENDING YOUR UNCONSCIOUSNESS

any steps actually creates an altogether different path, and therefore, a different destination.

The process must begin with *"Ending Your Unconsciousness,"* which is a journey through this endless lacking that has permeated your existence into something that leaves you seeing the potential before you. It is a necessary beginning for the realisation to occur, and that leads to the discovery of your very own power. We work through the basics, to lay a foundation in rocky soil and plant our crop; but to do so, we must first clear a space for peace and forgiveness to create the necessary understanding for change to feel at home.

We then move towards your awakening in *"Awakening to Your Truth."* This is specifically designed to challenge your belief systems to help you understand that these old belief systems that you hold so very dear to your heart, that you protect at all costs, are no longer working for you. This doesn't mean you must adopt *my* belief systems, but it is an example to understand why you need to reset and find a new set of beliefs to build the new "you" upon.

Although you have already been manifesting your life, I will show you how to manifest a better life, a happier, more fulfilling life, and hopefully, the life you have desired for so long. I show you that through *"Manifesting Your Journey,"* where you can

INTRODUCTION

create whatever you seek in your heart. I walk you through each of the steps necessary to get you there. The work is yours to undertake as the journey is yours too. It cannot be done by anyone else, and if you are serious about the much-desired change in your life, you will do what it takes to ensure you achieve what you have long desired.

While working through the processes, *"Accepting Your Success,"* is essential to clearing the blockages you once held so dearly, albeit unconsciously. We delve into the depths of your life creation through the analysis of success and what it all means to you. It is okay to have a different idea of success to me or to others, but finding what success means to you is an important part of the journey you are undertaking. You will learn that *being* is more important than *doing*, and through living the new you, you will learn how to become what you set out to be.

"Creating Your Destiny" brings it all together. This is where the road widens, where you gather speed, and with a little more pressure on the throttle, you feel the wind in your hair and weightlessness of possibility lift you up far beyond what you could have possibly imagined. This is where the New You is created. This is where we deal with the roadblocks that eventually come before you, and why (and how) everything we have learned all comes together.

ENDING YOUR UNCONSCIOUSNESS

The path I set before you is not an easy one. It is also not a quick one, but it is a successful one. The work that needs to be done is about self-reflection and personal growth. It is about challenging your long-held beliefs, wrestling with your ego, and finding the place in your heart where Love beats the strongest. It may take days, weeks or months, as it is up to you, the individual, to explore. We all start from different places, spaces and times in our life, where life is either complex or simple. But either way, the process works for all those who are willing to do the work. Tried and true across many who have worked with me individually, it is now available to you.

Of course, it is easier to complete the journey with a helping hand, and someone to keep you accountable. It is also expensive, and not something everyone has access to. Now you do. But it will never change what is required, and it will never change the work that needs to be done, because it is your journey to make, your work to undertake.

We all have a place in the Universe, and yours is here, at this point in time, listening to these words. In time, you will be listening to another's words, and another's, as you seek and strive for more and more personal growth and direction. I hope to ignite a passion for finding your truth - not only for finding it in these words, but for seeking it out from the wide Universe and

INTRODUCTION

the many souls of inspiration that lie within. Life is but a blessing, to behold and wonder. It is not for the suffering or for the wanting; for the soul wants nothing from life but for life to just *be*.

This is your journey, and only you can take it, for it is for none other than yourself to create this life, long-lasting and fulfilling…

…and your journey begins with consciousness.

Chapter One

My Truth Does Not Have to Be Your Truth

What is the Truth? I don't know about you, but I've been searching for the Truth for a very large part of my life and I'm not too sure whether I know exactly what the Truth is.

You see, the Truth (and the way we perceive it) is very much based on our experience; and our experience - how we were raised, the environment that we were brought up in, our friends, our family, our peers, the people we look up to - shapes our perspective and how we view life.

Any policeman will tell you that if you are interviewing ten people at the scene of an accident, only a few items within what they say might actually correlate; everything else is just a matter of perspective and viewpoint. Our perspective is shaped by our beliefs, our attitude, how we're feeling on any given day, and even our emotional and physical state. Ten people can see the same event many different ways; and worse still, they can explain it in many more ways than they initially experienced it.

The Truth is very subjective. There may be my Truth and there may be your Truth. Ultimately speaking, is there a single Truth?

Some of us talk about the fact that God is a single point of Truth. I believe that Love is the single point of Truth. Ultimately, as God is Love, I guess I'm speaking the same language. However, isn't Truth created through the perspective of the viewing, and since perspective is such an individual experience, wouldn't Truth then be subjective and not exclusive? I mean, we humans cannot even agree on what God is. We can't even decide on which God we are giving our attention to, as a singularity or as a group consciousness. So how could we possibly agree on something as complex as Truth?

The only way I can surmise what Truth is, is to consider it as an individual viewpoint, based on personal perspective; and that one person's Truth doesn't need to be another person's Truth. In

CHAPTER ONE

fact, I believe there actually doesn't need to be a single, definitive Truth at all.

The reason why I'm talking to you about the Truth is I want to be really clear about something before we get started. I want to get a message across to you about the fact that I actually don't expect my Truth to be your Truth. All I desire is for you to figure out what your Truth is.

I have a broader understanding of what my Truth is these days. I obtained this perspective through re-examining my belief system and looking at the rules at play in my life. Also, looking at my past perspective and trying to figure out which experience has led to that perspective and how that influences the way that I view things. I believe this is important if we want to understand why we view the Truth to be a certain way.

We talk about the fact that our eyes are viewers - but they're also projectors, in the way that we project our perspective of life onto the experience that we have, and into the experience of others. This is particularly true if we then talk to someone about that perspective, giving them an idea of what we've experienced or telling them about how we feel about something. Just because I say something that is coming from my Truth or from my heart, it doesn't necessarily mean it has to be your Truth, and that is my point.

ENDING YOUR UNCONSCIOUSNESS

I think part of the problem is that there are a lot of spiritual teachers that talk about concepts or theories as being black and white, when in fact, nothing in the Universe and certainly nothing in our overall experience, either collectively or singularly, is black and white. Life is not designed to be, nor supposed to be experienced as, anything like a black or white experience. It is only ever made of our individual and collective life experience, and the perspective that we develop as a result of that life experience.

We all come from different perspectives and from different upbringings. If you analyse some twins, and you put them in the same family with the same upbringing by the same parents, and send them to the same school, they will still have different thoughts, feelings and belief systems. They will grow up to be very, very different people on the inside, even if they look and behave similarly on the outside. To me, I think that's an exciting thing. I think that's a wonderful part of being human and what being human is all about: our uniqueness and individuality.

We have the right to have our own belief system and we have the right to our own thoughts. We are allowed to create our life experience based not only on our past but also on what we truly desire for our future. This is what ultimately determines our perspective that influences our Truth.

CHAPTER ONE

However, I believe we need to be careful, because knowing your Truth is one thing, but imposing your Truth on people is actually an act of judgement. From my perspective, my Truth doesn't have to be your Truth, in the same way that your Truth doesn't have to be mine. I hope that you listen to some of the things that I say and take them on board (as you may do with other people) and do your own exploration, your own research and make up your own mind based on what your Truth is or may become.

I think ultimately that's all we can do, and a lot of us are on this path or journey to find our Truth. We soak up information from a whole range of different people, different sources and through different mediums; and we take on board that information to see how it correlates within us. For a lot of people, if they are working from a low vibrational frequency, they struggle to understand concepts and ideas that come from a source of high vibrational frequency, and they dismiss it as nonsense or rubbish, and that is O.K. with me, because it is their choice, to create their life as they see fit, even if they are doing it unconsciously. It always is their choice, and their choice alone.

Have you ever been in a situation where you're trying to impart some wisdom or some teaching, or trying to get someone to see a particular perspective, and they're just not getting it? It's

ENDING YOUR UNCONSCIOUSNESS

falling on deaf ears? Partly, that's because not everybody is in the same space at the same time - and I don't mean in a physical sense, I mean in a spiritual sense. In a frequency sense.

Not all of us are able to understand what's going on. Sometimes, when we are imparting our Truth or sharing our Truth, we need to be careful that we're not evangelising our version of the Truth because it may not necessarily be someone else's Truth. If we're evangelising and we're pushing it and we're forcing it onto other people, we need to respect that they also have a right to have their own belief system, their own thought structures and their own Truth. We shouldn't judge them for having an alternate perspective, viewpoint or belief system. Even if, in our own opinion, it is not working for them.

I honestly would love it if you listened to my teachings and it led you down a path and on a journey all of your own. In some ways, you may even disprove some of my Truths in searching for and finding your own Truth. For me, this is not about me being right and anybody else being wrong. In all honesty, it's about enabling people to embark on their journey, to take the path that best suits them, for the life experience that they desire to experience.

Truth, I think, is a very subjective word and there is no black and white in regard to Truth. We talk about it in a very idealistic

CHAPTER ONE

sense but there is always more than one perspective on any given event, through any given belief system, on any given experience.

There is always more than one perspective and as a result, there will actually be different versions of whatever the Truth may be for different people because the way we experience things is true to us. The way someone else experiences things is true to them. Sometimes they work, synchronise or correlate. Other times, they don't at all and we also need to honour and respect that, in the way we may wish others to honour our right to think and feel as we choose.

Within these pages I will seek to challenge your belief system. Please understand it is not done through judgement, but merely to get you to think more broadly about the possibilities of what is happening around you.

Please, sit back and relax, grab a hot cup of your favourite beverage, and enjoy the journey; because at times, I guarantee you: it is going to get a little weird.

Chapter Two

Why Do Some Teacher's Words Resonate?

Have you ever wondered why, when someone is talking to you about something, sharing their thoughts, feelings, experiences or talking about theories, ideals or wonderful things about how the universe works, the words really resonate with you and it feels really good inside you - yet you may not even fully understand the content?

Have you ever wondered why you relate better to what some people are saying, yet what others are saying is abrasive to you? Well, I get this question quite often. I get a lot of people wondering why, with certain spiritual teachers in their life, they just can't get enough of them and they listen to them over and over again. The words just absorb into their soul. They have videos that they watch, or audio tracks that they listen to, from certain spiritual teachers, playing almost on repeat cycle, over and over again. That is because the individual is listening to the words that the teacher is saying, and how they are saying it, and it genuinely resonates with them, as their own Truth at the level of the soul.

Other people can have a completely different experience. Some people don't like listening to people of the opposite sex. Some people don't like listening to people with different or difficult-to-understand accents. Some don't like listening to people who are too technical, or too academic in their delivery. In fact, a room full of people can all listen to the same words, and some will hail it as the most important thing they have ever heard, and others will argue that it is complete rubbish. It's the same words, same delivery and same environment. It doesn't mean what is being said is any less the Truth, it just doesn't necessarily resonate with the individual at the same level they are seeking. So, I want to talk to you about why that is the case.

Why is it that certain people really resonate with you and what they say really resonates with you as your own Truth, even if they're dealing with concepts that are so outside your understanding at this current point in time? Well, a lot of it

CHAPTER TWO

comes down to energy, and the frequency that energy offers.

Everything we are, and everything all around us, is energy. Our energy carries with it a certain vibrational frequency that helps us interact with the things around us. This is explained by the understanding that you have walked into a place before, or walked into a room full of people and sometimes, when you've done that, you feel energised. You feel excited, really pumped up and happy to be there. Well, ultimately, what's happening is you're feeling the energy within the collective group and their energy is matching the energetic frequency you are desiring.

The same concept is happening when you walk into a room and it doesn't feel right. You feel uneasy about being there, or unsafe, and you cannot get out of there fast enough. In fact, it feels awful to experience, and you can feel a hole or an emptiness in your stomach that causes you to sit back and think, "I really don't want to be in this space." This is actually due to incompatible energetic frequencies. Your energetic frequency is higher or lower than the other frequencies within the room, and they clash. One is not necessarily better than the other, it's just that they are incompatible, which creates the tension and unease.

If you have ever been to an Eckhart Tolle conference you would feel the powerful energy in the room. Just being in the vicinity of the hall that he's in, with thousands of people there to

ENDING YOUR UNCONSCIOUSNESS

experience his energy and his teachings, is deliciously intoxicating. You don't even have to go inside to experience it. It is this beautiful, emotional experience that can only be felt and not easily described. Similar to a Tony Robbins event, when there's 25,000 people in the entertainment centre and they're all jumping up and down and getting excited, and he's pumping you all up, and the energy in the room is inescapably incredible. The same thing happens when you get home and your partner's feeling really flat, your kids are running amok or you walk into the office and something just doesn't feel quite right, your energy is up, and their energy is down. What is happening is the same, albeit felt in different ways. This is because energy is contagious - yours, and everyone else's.

What is happening is your field of energy, and the way you operate your field of energy is either compatible with the energy around you, (therefore giving you a pleasurable, happy experience) or incompatible against the type of energy around you. The vibrational energy is best described as a range from a low vibrational frequency to a high vibrational frequency. Low frequencies are associated to negative thoughts like guilt, shame, hate, and anger. High vibrational frequencies are associated to positive thoughts of Love, peace, and joy to name a few. So, when you're in a happy, joyful, loving space and you walk into a room

CHAPTER TWO

with a bunch of people that really don't want to be there, or they've just had a negative experience, you will feel that energetic difference. We all do. Some of us are more aware, more attuned to it; and others are more unconscious to it. Either way, it is always there, but our level of conscious awareness towards it is different.

Now, the interesting thing is how we also experience energies when we are talking to people. I'm sure all the ladies out there have had the experience of when they're in a particular space, like a bar, or a pub, or club, and they can feel a leering energy of some creepy guy that won't really give them enough space or is constantly trying to get into a conversation with them that they don't feel comfortable about. All you can think about, at that particular time, is, "How on earth do I get out of here?" The same experience happens with people in our life that are trying too hard to be our friend or trying too hard to be intimate with us - even if we know them well, like a husband or wife. Sometimes our energies just don't match in a given moment.

It's exactly the same thing with spiritual teachers. It's the same thing with anybody that you are seeking guidance from, like counsellors, psychologists and social workers. If your energy feels good in their space, e.g., they're not coming from a negative, fear-constructed type energy like judgement, or they are coming from

ENDING YOUR UNCONSCIOUSNESS

a Love-constructed energy like compassion and joy or happiness, you can understand how that would feel very, very different.

You and your soul are very much as one. A lot of people think that we are our bodies, when we're not. We are the soul that resides within the body. The soul knows and understands what universal Truth is. When a spiritual teacher explains their version (or their filtered version) of what the universal Truth is, and it resonates with you, your soul is reacting to that information. Your heart expands. Your soul goes, "Oh, this is fabulous. I've been waiting to hear something like this for a long time" in the hope that it wakes us up to our ongoing purpose of why we came here, or to our own conscious connection.

The energy created in the words that have been spoken, and in the way that they are being spoken, is ultimately what you are resonating with. It's what your heart is feeling. However, if we are caught in an Ego-driven mindset, woke up on the wrong side of bed, or our day's just gone south for whatever reason, we're not necessarily going to be at the frequency we need to be to be able to hear some type of remarkable, spiritual truth, now are we?

What we need to think about is: when we're in that particular state and we want to be in a higher vibrational state, we need to become aware of the need to change our state. We can get up out of our chair and go for a walk. I used to grab my secateurs

CHAPTER TWO

and my hedge clippers, and I would go out in the garden and tend to my plants. Being in the space of my plants, and giving them a haircut, enjoying the space, and cutting some flowers always got me out of my negative, low-vibrational state and brought me into a much higher-vibrational state. It's not hard to understand why being in the company of pure presence helps us become more present. It is as infectious as a good laugh or a beautiful heart driven smile. To find presence, some may go for a walk, go fishing or even find a good friend to have a chat with. The activity isn't important; what is important is that it makes you feel good, it brings you peace and helps you connect with whatever makes you genuinely happy.

So, when someone's talking to you, and they're sharing their thoughts and feelings from their heart, it is ultimately coming through a model of inspiration from their soul, their higher self, their spirit guides (depending on whatever your belief system is) – or from their God. When that discussion is coming from the heart and you are feeling that, and it's really resonating with you, what is happening is you are experiencing their words as your Truth. Your energetic frequencies are aligning. You don't have to understand the concepts. You don't have to understand the science behind it. You don't have to understand any of that, you just feel it, and it resonates with you. It almost gives you a bit of

ENDING YOUR UNCONSCIOUSNESS

thirst, saying, "I want to go and find out what this evolutionary theory is about," or, "I want to go and find out what these spiritual teachings are about," or any other wonderful theories or concepts that they are talking about. When that vibrational energy fits yours as Truth, it sends you on an energetic path of exploration and spiritual adventure.

This happens when your heart, or your soul, has heard an element of what it knows to be universal Truth which comes from the soul's connection to all and everything that is. So, don't be afraid to listen to another's words. They're just discussions. It's just dialogue. All you're doing is listening to what they have to say. It cannot do you any harm and it may change your life for the better. As the old saying goes: "Once the student is ready, the teacher arrives." Anyone can be your teacher. For me, it is my partner, my kids and sometimes those who attack me. Everyone can teach you something.

If you are clicking on a particular YouTube link, reaching out for a particular book at the bookstore, or grabbing some information off the Internet, it's very likely your inspired soul is trying to provide an opportunity for personal growth and learning. The universe has provided an opportunity for you to change your perspective, and perhaps change your belief system to move forward with a slightly different perspective that is

CHAPTER TWO

healthier and Love-driven, rather than Egoic and Fear-driven.

Sometimes, as we take off on our spiritual path, we have everything ignited with excitement from our own particular spiritual teacher, but then we outgrow that spiritual teacher. It's not because you're becoming more spiritual than them or you're higher up some spiritual evolutionary ladder or anything like that. It doesn't work that way.

What it means is that you've heard what you needed to hear. Don't be afraid to then go on and find another type of spiritual teacher or someone who can give you a different type of personal guidance, because their energy might be what you need to hear and feel at that particular time. You may come back to the original teacher, and if you need to that is always O.K. You might end up by having a dozen teachers over a number of years, if not decades.

Sometimes it's really healthy to get different perspectives on things. This is what I try and do with everybody who I end up working with. I say to them that my Truth isn't necessarily their Truth and I don't expect it to be; and in fact, I don't necessarily want it to be. I want you to find your own Truth and your Truth mechanism is all about how it feels. It's all about how your heart feels when it is hearing the words and feeling the delivery of those words. It is about how you feel when you are in the space of

ENDING YOUR UNCONSCIOUSNESS

another. Then you can decide what you want to do with that new-found information you have heard.

Just because I believe something, doesn't mean everybody else has to. But I do hope; and the reason why I am working with you is in the hope that the words that you find within these pages could just trigger some areas of curiosity in you, so that you can get excited about life again and start to make some of the changes that you have desired for so very long.

I hope you find that opportunity and that you can find meaning in what I am saying, or in what other people are saying, to try and then establish what your new belief system may be, what your new Truth is; and try and use that as an opportunity to get excited and start creating the incredible life that you were born to live.

Chapter Three

Love and Fear

Everything we experience is based on one of two things. Every thought, every feeling, every choice we make is based on either Love or Fear.

What I mean is that at its root cause, everything that happens to us, in our life, in our work, with our families, in our interactions with others, even in sitting in our own private space - everything that happens in our experience is based on either Love or Fear.

The exciting thing is that we have a choice to determine which experience is based on Love and which experience is based on Fear. The ultimate free will, if you like. Most people who live in their heads a lot are usually run by the monkey mind, as the Buddhists call it; or the endless chatter that goes on, almost like

ENDING YOUR UNCONSCIOUSNESS

the parrot that sits on your shoulder, constantly talking trash in your ear. A lot of that is actually driven by the Ego, Fear's foot soldier.

Fear is quite a destructive thing, because for Fear to maintain its own relevance, it must disconnect and destroy you. It only wants to put you down and make you feel bad. Sometimes, to be really clever, the Ego might also build you up, for the purpose of separating you from others, setting you apart from others, or to get you thinking that you are better than them. Fear only disconnects and pulls things apart. Fear disintegrates things and is very destructive. But Fear is also very, very clever.

The Ego, Fear's foot soldier, works tirelessly to try and make sure that it maintains its own relevance, and that it maintains control of you, its host. Now, this Love and Fear dichotomy is a very powerful mechanism at play in our life, when we start to understand it. The problem is that most of us actually live a highly unconscious existence. We are not aware that we have the ability to create our own life experience, or that we can control our life experience. Once we start to better understand that we have this choice available to us, we can start to understand to what level we can create our own life.

If every thought, every feeling, every choice we make is actually based on Love or Fear, then why wouldn't we make every

CHAPTER THREE

choice based on Love? To be clear, what I mean by Love, is not the Twilight, romantic, teenage sense of the word "Love." I mean that Love is everything that is positive in your life and Fear is everything that is negative in your life. Love is creative, expansive, joyful and peaceful. Love connects people and builds people up. Love enables people to help others out of difficult situations or encourages someone to do something nice for someone else.

Love gives us thoughts of joy and happiness and Love gives us ideas of great things that we want to do. Love is ultimately where our inspiration comes from. Inspiration talks only through a language of Love, and that comes through the heart.

Fear has a negative language - the language spoken through the Monkey Mind. Fear is the language spoken by the Ego. As complete opposites, Love cannot speak through constructs of Fear and Fear cannot speak through constructs of Love. For example, let's think about things like honesty. Is honesty a construct of Love, or is it a construct of Fear? Well, to me that seems fairly obvious. Honesty is a construct of Love. So, in turn, dishonesty, or lies are constructs of Fear. Now, if the Ego can only speak a language of Fear, and Fear is only a language of dishonesty, then the untruths and lies spoken through Fear, spoken through the Ego, cannot possibly be true.

ENDING YOUR UNCONSCIOUSNESS

Some people ask, "How do we tell the difference between the Ego talking and our inspiration talking?" I believe it's all about how it feels. I believe that when Fear and the Ego are in place, the way we feel is really negative. We feel really down. We feel destructive, angry, narcissistic, we feel egoic; all these really nasty things about the way we want to treat people or what we want to do, come to mind. That is ultimately the way it makes us feel, even if it might make us feel powerful to separate us from people. It still doesn't feel very nice. It never does in comparison to how Love makes us feel.

When Love is at play, Love feels fabulous. It is calm. It is respectful. It is quiet. Love is everything that we could possibly want in our lives that is good for us. So, if Fear is everything negative, and Love is everything positive, think about it for a second. The Fear and the Ego and the lies that the Ego tells us separates us from others. It's what causes wars. It is what destroys relationships. Why? Why would Fear be even remotely interested in that? Ultimately, it wants to maintain its own relevance. You see, I believe that we incarnate onto this beautiful planet so we can experience everything that life has to offer - and what life has to offer is both Love and Fear. We actually come here to experience things that are negative, that are difficult, that are trials and tribulations in our lives. We come here to actually

CHAPTER THREE

experience suffering. Why? Because we cannot experience it in the spiritual state.

The thought process then is: if we come here and we have all this negativity happening, how is it necessarily our choice? Why do we have a choice? Well, I believe we have a choice because we actually come here to experience and to transcend Fear. I believe we come here to overcome Fear and to evolve as a spiritual being, to evolve as a human being, and to realise that Love, ultimately speaking, is all we really need.

Now, you're probably sitting back thinking, "Well, that's all very easy and good and well for you to say." Maybe. I've been doing this for some time. Maybe I've got lots of practice at it. But look, to be honest, it's not easy for anybody. As anyone who understands the concepts of this and has practised it for a long time knows, it's not easy. It wasn't easy for me. It's just in hindsight everything seems easier than it ever was. Tony Robbins, Wayne Dyer and Richard Branson make success look easy, but it was only born through three or four decades of hard work by them. Really personal work, on themselves, each and every day. It isn't easy, but it is most certainly worth it. The reason why it isn't easy is primarily because we have been living in an egoic state for so long, we honestly don't know anything different. We have forgotten what living in a present state is. This

ENDING YOUR UNCONSCIOUSNESS

is mainly because the Ego will never let up; it will always fight to maintain control. The Ego may have you think that you have the Ego beaten, but to be quite honest with you, whenever I've thought that, that's usually the Ego just telling me that so that I drop my guard. But what we need to do is to first of all recognise what's happening within us, recognise the Ego for what it is and for how it presents in our Life Experience.

Call the Ego out. Say, "Hello, Ego. I can see you there. I can hear you chattering in my mind." By recognising the Ego, we can then start to make a differentiation about the fact that everything the Ego is telling us is false. Why? Because the Ego can only speak the language of Fear, and dishonesty, untruths and lies - all of them are part of that language of Fear. If the Ego was to tell the truth, it would almost destroy itself, because using a language of Love would set it apart from Fear - and that's not what it wants to do. The Ego wants to maintain control of its host, and it can only do that through using Fear.

So, in recognising the Ego, and the way the Ego rises up within us, we can then start to reflect on what we desire as an alternative experience. Do we actually want to continue to be unconscious? Do we want to continue to be a person who is ruled by the Ego? Do we want to continue to be a person who is ruled by the negative thoughts of others, thoughts of judgement, and

CHAPTER THREE

complain about everything else that's going on around us and in our lives?

Well, I don't. I actually want to be recognised as a person who loves. I want to be recognised as a person who is happy and joyful and peaceful. I actually want happiness in my life. So, for me, I need to first of all recognise that the Ego is present; recognise what the Ego is trying to do. Now at first - and this is what slowed me down - for years I would tell the Ego to go away. I'd get angry at the Ego and say, "Leave me alone," but then I started to realise I was giving it the same energy that created it. I was being angry at the Ego, and anger is a construct of Fear. So, in thinking through this a little bit further, I started to realise that if I want to transcend Fear, if I want to transcend the darkness that comes with Fear, ultimately, I need to switch on the light. I need to give it Love. I need to offer it Love; and sure enough, it happened. Offering Fear Love, offering the Ego Love, makes it disappear.

So now, I say, "Hello Ego. Thanks for coming back. It's really good to see you again but thank you. I don't want to hear your lies. I don't need your lies and I don't believe what you are saying. I'm O.K. I can make my own decisions about this situation."

This is best done through my "Recognise, Reflect and Resolve" process, that I discuss in detail in my first book, *Free*

ENDING YOUR UNCONSCIOUSNESS

from Fear. In any given situation, we first need to *Recognise* what is happening within us, or within others. Then we need to *Reflect* on what alternative life experience we desire in any given situation. Finally, we need to *Resolve* it by taking the action necessary to make the required change. So, by offering Love to the Ego, we are not only Recognising that the Ego is there, we are Reflecting that we want something other than that negative experience, and we are Resolving it through taking action. It really works. Because light dispels darkness, consciousness enlightens unconsciousness, and Love transcends Fear.

It really is that simple.

Chapter Four

We Create Our Own Life Experience

There is one thing that every successful person in the world knows: that we create our own life experience. Everything that we understand and experience in our life is a creation of our own thoughts and feelings. Every thought, every feeling and every choice we make is based on one of two things: Love or Fear. When I started to break that down, I began to realise that most of my life up until that point had actually been chosen based on constructs of Fear. Now, yes, that might have been unconscious on my behalf; but when I started to wake up to what was actually going on, I started to realise that my Ego ruled my life experience.

ENDING YOUR UNCONSCIOUSNESS

The Ego created my life experience for me. The Ego is a foot soldier of Fear and the Ego can only speak a language of Fear, which means my life experience was certainly more negative than it needed to be. Now, I haven't had the hardest life, at all. I haven't come from extreme poverty, extreme disease or been really downtrodden. When I changed my perspective on things and started actively choosing constructs of Love in my life, my life experience changed.

A lot of people then immediately jump in with the question "Well, hold on a second. We can't control what happens to us." Well, maybe we can't. Maybe we can't control what happens to us because, from time to time, someone is going to do something to harm us, or say something to hurt us. However, the one thing we can control (which is completely within our control) is our reaction to what happens to us. You see, what people do to us is actually a reflection of them, not us at all. How we react to them and to their actions, or how we react to things that have happened to us, is a reflection of us. If we are living in a state where the Monkey Mind and the Ego has control over our daily thought processes, the experiences we get out of it will be highly negative.

What we need to do is recognise the Ego and transcend the Ego through a process of offering the Ego Love. I have managed to do this over a period of time. I'm not saying I'm perfect at it, because the Ego is very clever and likes to sneak in every now and then. What I am saying is: I've learnt to choose constructs of Love by changing some of my belief systems, and by changing some of my experiences through those belief systems. This gives me a more positive life experience.

One of the beliefs I had to change was the belief that we don't have the ability to create our own life experience. Now, this is a really big realisation for a lot of people, and I promise you that it is the truth. You are the only creator of your life experience. I would go so far as to say you are the only being in the entire universe that can create your life experience.

What do I mean by life experience? Well, it's fairly straightforward. Your life experience is everything you experience as life throughout each and every day. Most of us live life in an unconscious way. We're not conscious of everything going on around us. We're not conscious of our thoughts and feelings, and we're certainly not conscious of the choices we're making that reflect on that experience. Through following the process of Recognise, Reflect and Resolve, I first look to Recognise everything that's going on around me. What is happening to me? Why is it happening to me? Why are my thoughts about it negative or positive in any given situation? By

ENDING YOUR UNCONSCIOUSNESS

looking at these things, analysing them and Recognising things for what they are, we can move from a place of being unconscious into a state of conscious awareness.

Through that state of awareness, we can begin to understand exactly what's going on around us. We can begin to understand that life does not happen *to* us, but that life happens *for* us. I see the universe as a big mirror. I see that the universe, and the life it enables, are both here to actually reflect back to us what we choose to create as our life experience. I've always been a relatively proactive and a reasonably happy fellow. But what I wasn't doing was consciously choosing success, consciously choosing abundance, and consciously choosing happiness. What I didn't realise was that by consciously choosing Love constructs to be part of my life experience, my life experience would change dramatically.

I decided a number of years ago that I wanted to change who I was. That was driven by the boys that I have in my life, my kids. I realised that I wasn't being the father that I wanted them to grow up with. I've always been a person that actually chooses to lead by example, so why not with Fatherhood? What was happening was I was unconsciously leading by an example I was not happy with. Once I became conscious of what was going on around me I started to realise that I needed to make better choices - and I wanted to make better choices for me. I wanted to make better choices for my family. The beautiful thing that happened as a result of that is my Fear of a whole range of different things had fallen away as a result of those choices. It's not actually because the physical world has changed around me. It's my perspective of my physical world that is changing. So, by looking at the fact that life doesn't happen *to* us, life happens *for* us, we can literally create a life of abundance. We can create a life of success.

I set about, for many years, to try and analyse this - to break it all down and try to understand. If I'm going to go from the person that I was, to the person that I really desired to be, how do I make that transition? A lot of that was about Recognising what was happening to me at any given moment; Reflecting on what I chose in return and choosing Love and Love-based constructs to enter my Life Experience; then Resolving it by taking action.

Now, the action is the important bit; because without action, we can't actually get anywhere. We can't do anything. We can't implement change. With action, though, we need to be sure of what it is we actually desire - and that's why the Reflect stage in the "Recognise, Reflect and Resolve" process is very important. Without Reflecting and making a conscious choice about what we desire in our experience, we don't know what action we need

ENDING YOUR UNCONSCIOUSNESS

to take to Resolve it.

We don't always know what action we have to take but we usually can figure out the first step, or the first two steps, that need to be taken in regard to the action. Once we've Recognised what we desire, we need to get on and take that action so that we can start creating that life experience. When we do this, we send a signal out the Universe, and with the Universe being a mirror, it then reflects back that intention to us and helps us create the next step, the next action, whatever is needed to Resolve it. Part of this can be done through conscious association with our inspiration and a conscious disassociation with our Ego.

Ultimately speaking, it comes through practice and patience. You are not going to be able to switch the Ego off just like that. You are also not going to be able to turn your life around just like that. But there is one thing you can do: you *can* turn around your thought processes *just like that*. You can make a decision now, at any point in time, to hit the Reset Button to make that change. To me, that was defining and reflecting on who it was that I desired to be. I desired to be a better father. I desired to be a better lover. I desired to be better friends to the people that I associated with and a better leader to the world. I desired to help people and give back to the world. So, you can see that I was choosing a whole range of Love-constructed forces that I desired to implement in my life.

None of them were negative in nature. Most of them were about helping others. By hitting that Reset Button, I was taking the definition that I had put together of who I desired to be, and I was saying, in a statement to myself and to the Universe, that I am no longer the person of the past. I am no longer the person who is caught up in my Ego. I am no longer the person who is caught up in that Fear-contained state. I am a person who is going to create a life of Fear-free abundance and a person who is going to love people through Love-based constructs.

Now, that Reset Button was a really important turning point for me because it empowered me to make some significant changes in my life that were absolutely necessary. I can promise you: to this day, people around me see me not only as a very different person - they don't see me as the old person anymore. They also see the benefits that come from me being this person that I've chosen to create. Now, part of my life, and part of what I am choosing to do, is to try and share all of these things with you.

My goal is to help those that seek help to change themselves, to change their lives, and to change their relationships. Once we make those changes, we can start creating a life we only ever dared dream about.

I promise you: there is no better feeling than living the life,

ENDING YOUR UNCONSCIOUSNESS

day-to-day, that you have only ever dreamt about. You pinch yourself every day because living the dream is what we are born to do.

Chapter Five

Your Ego

If someone was talking to you, and they were being honest with you, would that be a language of Fear or would that be a language of Love? That would be a construct of Love. Honesty is a construct of Love. But lies and deceit? They're definitely a construct of Fear. Now, the Ego can't do anything on the basis of Love. The Ego can't offer anything that's constructed of Love because that would make the Ego completely irrelevant. The Ego is controlled by Fear, and the Ego wants to control you through constructs of Fear. Anger, frustration, discontent, disconnection, separation, judgement, complaining... I could go on and on and on. We all live it, day-to-day. Complaining, judging ourselves and others, living in a constant state of drama.

ENDING YOUR UNCONSCIOUSNESS

We all live it until we choose *not* to.

The Ego is a very crafty beast. In fact, the Ego in the most part has been smarter than you or I have been to date. I say that because we, for the most part, are not even aware of the fact that the Ego exists, let alone the fact that the Ego controls us through our everyday lives. The biggest trick the Ego has ever played is to have us believe that we are *it*. It's thoughts, it's manipulations.

Now, what if I were to tell you that everything negative that you have heard about everybody else is also a lie? The reason why I'm saying that is because it's the Ego that tells you everything negative about everybody else, and everything the Ego tells you is a lie.

The big thing that the Ego managed to get us to believe is that everything that goes on around us is actually about *us*, when it really isn't. Think of it this way. If we are all so self-centred and thinking it is all about us, then who is it really about? We think everyone else is judging us, talking about us, and that everything they do is about us, when it is not. People are only thinking about themselves. This is the power of the Ego. It disconnects us by having us think only about ourselves, while it tells us that the rest of the world revolves around us. If everyone is thinking about themselves, no one is thinking about anyone else, and therefore no one is thinking about us at all. People are so caught up in

CHAPTER FIVE

managing their own day-to-day struggles that no one has time to be really all that concerned about everyone else. We need to stop worrying that the world is watching us and judging us. We need to remember that our thoughts are a reflection of us, not of anyone else.

If a person is angry at the office, our first instinct is to think, "Oh my God, what have I done?" When it's usually not about us at all. If there's someone driving slowly in the traffic, our first thought is, "That person is trying to slow me down." When that's not it at all. We are led to believe by the Ego that we are the centre of the whole universe, when we really aren't. I'm not saying we're not special. I'm not saying we're not loved. We are. Of course we are. What I'm trying to say is that we need to switch off from the Ego and we need to stop believing its rubbish.

Now, you might say, "How do I do that? How do I stop the Ego if I'm not even aware of where it is and how it's presenting in my life? How am I supposed to move forward?" Well, I'd like to say that it's really easy. The technique in itself is easy, but what's difficult (and a real challenge) is the regular application of that technique. Partly that's because the moment we Recognise the Ego, Reflect on what we want instead, and Resolve the Ego, the Ego is already thinking of changing its approach.

Again, the Ego is very, very clever. The Ego knows that if

ENDING YOUR UNCONSCIOUSNESS

you don't listen to the rubbish that it tells you (such as someone else is attacking you or saying nasty stuff about you) then it will rally other Egos and turn them against you and turn them against each other. Then it creates this whole witch hunt, where everybody grabs their pitchforks and their torches, and off they go to burn the witch. The Ego is a crafty beast, but it has one weakness - one very, very big weakness - and that is Love.

You see, Fear and darkness go hand in hand. Love and light also go hand in hand. Now, we all know that darkness cannot survive the presence of light. That is a beautiful analogy to describe the fact that Fear is weak and that Love is all-powerful. Fear cannot survive in the presence of Love. It's a simple fact and I ask anybody to prove otherwise. Fear is weak. Fear is the schoolyard bully. It is a coward with absolutely no confidence. Fear acts like it is strong, but if we remember carefully, Fear cannot tell the truth, which means its pretence of strength is nothing but a lie, as is every word it utters.

When we're thinking about the Ego, the first task I give people is to go through their day-to-day activities over the first few weeks and Recognise every single point in time when the Ego becomes present in their life - when the Ego gets into your ear and starts talking trash. Recognition of the Ego is half the battle. We need to see the Ego and how it presents so that we can make

CHAPTER FIVE

a choice that is alternative to that experience.

The Ego doesn't want to be Recognised. The Ego doesn't want us to know that it is there because only through Recognition of the Ego can we overcome it. While it hides in the shadows of your mind it can maintain control without you even knowing.

So think about the Ego. Think about every negative thought you have ever had. It might be thoughts about yourself. To be quite honest with you, most people (including myself) have negative thoughts about ourselves all the time. We think that we're fat. We think that we are not nice people. We think that people won't like us. We think that we're not capable, that we won't be able to do our job - a whole range of things. That is all the Ego at work.

Remember, the Ego can only speak a language of Fear. In the language of Fear, in the constructs of Fear, all there can be is dishonesty and lies. So, anything the Ego tells you is a complete lie and a fabrication. First, we must Recognise the Ego. We must find out when and how it's presenting. I always like to think about *why* it would be presenting in this particular way as well.

Through the years of practicing over and over again this same technique, I have realised that the Ego actually wants us to disconnect. It wants to separate us from the people around us

ENDING YOUR UNCONSCIOUSNESS

because when we're connected with people, that's when Love starts to come into play, that's when Love starts to triumph. And of course, the Ego is not interested in Love. So, we need to Recognise the Ego every time it comes up.

For me, sometimes it comes up in the traffic when someone's driving really slowly or weaving around all over the traffic and not paying attention. It just gets me somehow, and my Ego jumps in every single time. Sometimes when people just don't think about what they're saying, or sometimes when people are being nasty to other people, the Ego in me jumps in and gets a hold of me again. It has me judging those nasty people. But I need to Recognise that as the Ego presenting itself again.

Once we've learnt to Recognise the Ego in every situation, we then need to stop, think and Reflect on what it is we desire instead. What do we desire our life to be?

I don't desire to have a life filled with Ego, Fear, domination, anger, frustration, hate and all that sort of stuff. That's not who I choose to be. What I want is a life filled with Love and happiness, peace, abundance, joy and connection to all that is around me. I can't do that if I'm constantly disconnected through my Ego. I can't listen to my inspiration if my Ego is constantly yelling in my ear. Love, and the language of Love, comes through the heart. We call it our inspiration, but it's done in a beautiful, lovely, caring

CHAPTER FIVE

whisper in our ear - and Love cannot be heard clearly without making a choice to stop listening to the loud and overbearing Ego.

So, we Recognise the Ego and how it's presenting - and it will present in a million different ways. When we think we've figured it out, the Ego will tell us we have, and then it's got a hold of us again. Recognise how it's presenting. Reflect on what we want instead. And then, here's the kicker: what we need to do is to Resolve it.

Recognise, Reflect and Resolve.

We need to Resolve the situation, that negative experience that we're having through the Ego, and take action by offering Love to the Ego. We need to switch on the light in the presence of darkness. We need to offer Love because Love transcends Fear every time. The Ego cannot survive in the presence of Love.

So, I have a little mantra that I say over and over again. I say, "Thank you, Ego. I recognise your presence. I don't want your lies and deceit. I Love you. I got this." I say that over and over again, every time it comes up.

You may choose your own version of that mantra, and that's completely fine. The idea is: don't get *angry* at the Ego, because then you're adding the same energy that created the Ego in the first place. You need to Love the Ego. Don't encourage the Ego

ENDING YOUR UNCONSCIOUSNESS

but Love the Ego. "Thank you, Ego. I recognise your presence. I don't need your lies and deceit. I Love you. I got this" Then you go on your way.

Some days I feel like I've done it forty thousand times. It's all about the constant reapplication of this approach, and soon you begin to experience a certain freedom that comes from not being controlled by the Ego. The Ego becomes quieter and quieter each time you do this. Unfortunately, it's not going to give up. It's part of living in the physical life that we've chosen on this planet. However, it is something that can be slowly transcended over time. Eventually you will start to feel such joy and happiness because you won't be caught up in this spiral of judgement and complaining and hate and suffering, which is all caused by the Ego.

The constant reapplication of the Recognise, Reflect and Resolve process will get you to where you want to be. Every time.

You just have to do the work to achieve the results.

Chapter Six

The Universe is A Mirror

What happens to you does not determine the quality of your life. But how you react to what happens around you does. You see, a lot of people think that the Universe wields this big stick of Karma. You do something wrong and the Universe comes and swats you like a fly. The problem with that thought process is that it takes no responsibility for the fact that we are the creators of our life experience. If the Universe is punishing us it is not because of anyone else, or any outside influence. It is because of the choices we have made.

ENDING YOUR UNCONSCIOUSNESS

I'm not saying people create experiences that harm them. What I'm saying is that no matter what happens to us, we have a choice to make about whether we experience that as pleasure or pain. We can choose to see that experience as something negative, as something terrible, as something tragic; or, we can see it as an opportunity for personal and evolutionary spiritual growth.

Everything that happens to us is not a reflection of us. Some people say it is a reflection of what is going on *inside* of us, but not necessarily a reflection *of* us. The way I look at this is that we are the creators of our own life experience. We can create whatever life we choose to create. If we want to be successful, if we want to help people, if we want to be known as a philanthropist or a teacher, or if we want to be known as someone who's not very nice, they are all choices that we make and display through our thoughts, feelings and actions.

The Universe is a big mirror. It is not the big stick of justice that some people think it is. Karma is not about punishing you for the wrong things that you've done. The Universe doesn't judge you on what you are doing and what you are not doing. Karma is actually all about the reflection. If you put out negativity, if you put out anger, if you put out frustration, if you put out judgement, then yes, the Universe is going to reflect that

CHAPTER SIX

back on you.

It is part of that universal mechanism to help us understand exactly how others are feeling as a result of our thoughts, feelings and actions. However, if we actually do something really wonderful, if we do something really nice for someone, help someone, build someone up, teach or educate someone, that is reflected back on us. Successful people know that the quickest path to being successful is helping others achieve success. For example, a true leader is not someone who actually leads, it's someone who creates the most leaders.

What is happening is that the Universe is reflecting back an amplified signal, coming not just from the person who is creating those leaders or the person who is helping others achieve success, but also from other people who are achieving their success, attributing that success to themselves and to the person who showed them. That breeds, develops and amplifies the signal to the Universe, and the Universe reflects it back. What someone does to us is not a reflection of *us*. It is only a reflection of *them*. However, your reaction to what they do to you *is* a reflection of yourself.

I used to think that people were out to get me in the office, or that people were out to do me harm, deliberately making choices that were all about me.

ENDING YOUR UNCONSCIOUSNESS

And you know what? I couldn't have been more wrong. Our mind and our Ego want us to believe that everything that happens around us is all about *us*. Well, I'm happy to tell you that it's not the truth - because the Ego can't tell the truth, and because truth is a construct of Love, and the Ego can only operate under a construct of Fear. The simple fact of the matter is that just in the way that *we* think everything is about *us*, so everybody *else* is thinking everything is about *them*. It's part of this Egoic Monkey Mind that is so prevalent in today's society.

We are taught that we are separate. We are taught about disconnection. We are given tools like drugs, alcohol and addictive substances that actually are about disconnection at their core, about switching off from our troubles, and switching off from the people around us so we can just be on our own to wallow in our own misery. What people are doing to you is actually about *them*. It is their choice to act and to behave as they do.

Now, I believe that we all have a right to be able to choose the life we seek to experience. You see, I choose constructs of Love. When I thought about the type of person I wanted to be and the type of life that I wanted to lead, I chose Love. Love is loving. Love is compassionate. Love is considerate. Love isn't judgemental. What people do to you is *not* about you. Don't

CHAPTER SIX

think it is about you. Don't take it on board as a judgement of you. What people are doing is about them. *How you react to them is about you* - and that's something that you do fundamentally have a choice about.

I think one of the biggest issues that we have in society at the moment is that we all think that we need to judge; that we need to cast judgement on one another; that we need to take retribution for something that someone has said about us or done to us - or maybe something that someone has done wrong to someone we love dearly. I'm not saying don't stick up for the people you love, I'm not saying that at all. I'm saying: let's try and do it from a position of Love. Let's try and be compassionate to those that are around us that can't find Love in their hearts. Let's laugh for those who can't find something to laugh about in their day. That's what Love does, and the Universe is just this big, giant mirror. If you want to be happy, help make another happy. If you want to be successful, help make another successful. You are the creators of your life. This creation of your life is by choice, and you can choose whether you want to be in a position of Love or whether you want to be in a position of Fear. It is, and forever will be, your choice.

You see, Love is a wonderful thing - forever expanding. Love is a joyful thing that shares and brings joy to everybody else.

ENDING YOUR UNCONSCIOUSNESS

The interesting thing is that darkness cannot survive the presence of light and Fear cannot survive the presence of Love. When someone is attacking you, by attacking them back, by adding anger and frustration and judgement back to them, you are adding the same energy to it that created it. The same goes if someone is mistreating someone you know - hurting them, bullying them, saying nasty things about them. Your anger, your retribution, cannot dispel their Fear-based attack that they have chosen through their actions. Your anger only makes their Fear-based choices stronger. It justifies their behaviour. It makes that energy bigger. What we need to do is counteract that energy. We need to add the opposite energy to what's happening.

If someone is hating you, or attacking you, or dealing with their life experience in the actions they're taking as a result of Fear-based constructs, then what I believe we need to do is insert Love-based constructs into the mix. We need to love them back. We need to be compassionate. We don't know what battles these people are facing. We don't know what trials and tribulations are going on. We don't know how badly they are caught in their Ego, or how in control Ego and Fear is in their lives. It is not our place to judge them if they are unconscious about being caught in their Ego.

The vast majority of people that I come across are "in their

CHAPTER SIX

head." The vast majority of them are controlled by Fear, and by Fear's foot soldier, the Ego. I believe compassion is needed. I believe we need to Love people for what is happening. Do you know what happens in response? It changes them. They feel it. They usually are surprised about the fact that judgement, anger and frustration hasn't come back to them, and they start to question what they are doing.

Love is such a beautiful, remarkable and powerful thing, and the Universe is your mirror. If you are experiencing a lot of anger in your life and a lot of negativity, what you need to do is override it. You need to change its state. Find things in your life that you are grateful for and Recognise what is happening within you.

When I do this, my thought processes are similar to, "I'm feeling angry. I'm feeling frustrated." In Recognising that, we then need to Reflect on what it is we desire to happen instead. By thinking about that, we can think about what is happening from a state of calm and choose a Love-based construct to work with. Then we can Resolve it, and remember that the resolution is all about taking the appropriate action. Sometimes forgiveness is in order. Sometimes we need to remove judgement from the equation. In other words, remove Fear from the situation by adding Love.

ENDING YOUR UNCONSCIOUSNESS

When you start to do this, the signal you are sending to the Universe is one of Love. This is received by the Universe and reflected back to you. By actively changing Fear-based constructs into Love-based experiences, the Universe changes its response for everyone.

Love is a very simple choice. On the other side of Love is abundance and joy and peace and happiness and the life you only ever dreamed of. You just need to make a simple choice.

I believe you can make that choice - and I'm happy to show you how.

Chapter Seven

Judgement is Not Working for You

Judgement is not working for you. Your judgement of others is not working for you. Your judgement of yourself is not working for you. In fact, your judgement is only sending you backward. Judgement is fundamentally a construct of Fear. This is based on the fact that everything we experience in life, every thought, every feeling, every choice we make, is based on either one of two things: Love or Fear.

What is judgement?

Judgement is ultimately a Fear construct, designed by the Ego to disconnect us from everything around us. Society has developed in such a way that it is perceived to be good practice to

ENDING YOUR UNCONSCIOUSNESS

judge other people for the decisions and the choices they're making. We are judging people for how they drive in the traffic. We are judging people for the way they dress, the way they look, the way they talk. We've been judging based on the colour of their skin, or for their religious beliefs. The judgement we are giving is not working for us. It really isn't - and it is time for it to stop.

I used to be a highly judgemental person. Every now and then the Ego still tries to creep in and take control. However, I have denounced judgement, and as a result, my life has turned around. Judgement ultimately is about us using others as an explanation for why our life experience is not keeping up with our expectations. In fact, like all Fear constructs, it couldn't be more of a lie.

We are blaming others for what we choose to experience. Now, I'm not saying we choose for someone to wrong us. I'm not saying we choose for someone to harm us, to attack us either violently, psychologically or sexually. I'm not saying that. What I'm saying is that our experience of what is happening is our choice. We can choose to see things as either an attack, as a negative, as a biased judgement against ourselves, as someone doing something wrong; or, we can actually see it as an opportunity to choose Love. We can see it as an opportunity for

CHAPTER SEVEN

spiritual growth. We can see it as an opportunity for personal development or for evolutionary growth.

By judging others, we are blaming other people for our life not being happy, for our life not being successful, for our life not being as rewarding as we ideally want it to be.

As children we believe that the world is our oyster. We start to lose that perspective over time because we are taught by the adults in our lives that that isn't the case. Well, I'm here to tell you: I believe that belief system is wrong, and counterproductive to everything we are here to achieve. I believe the world *is* our oyster. In fact, I believe we are the creators of our life. I also believe that judgement sends us backward.

What someone does to you is not about you. It's not even a reflection of you. It is about them and a reflection of them. How you *respond* to that is a reflection of yourself. If you want to be a judgemental person, that is also your choice. I am happy to respect your choice in that matter. It is your life. You can choose how to create your life. However, what is going to happen as a result of that judgement is the universe, being a mirror, is going to reflect that back to you. The universe is going to send judgement back to you.

Usually, if you don't learn the lesson, and you don't take the opportunity to learn from it, the universe keeps turning up the

ENDING YOUR UNCONSCIOUSNESS

volume. It will keep getting worse until you get the message. Judgement is no different from complaining. Complaining, at its core, is judgement. Judgement, at its core, is Fear. So, complaining is also a Fear construct. Complaining is just complaining about other things. It's just judging other things, other people, other events, other groups for the reason we are failing to be happy within our own lives. This is because what is happening around us is not meeting the requirements set out by our own beliefs-based rule set.

Now, we need to take control of this. When people come to me, seeking help, seeking guidance to try and turn their lives around, the first lesson I give them is, "You need to stop judging." Stop judging others. Stop judging other things that are going on around you and most of all, stop judging yourself.

We are so good at judging ourselves. We judge ourselves because we're fat. We judge ourselves because we're ugly, because people don't like us, because we are not living the life we feel we should. But all of that is just simply not true. That is just the Ego in our head running a Fear-based dialogue. It's just the Ego carrying on, because the Ego wants to disconnect us from our brilliance. The Ego wants to disconnect us from those around us. The Ego wants to disconnect us from Love because the Ego knows that when we are connected to others, to our

CHAPTER SEVEN

magnificence, or to Love, the Ego has no place. In fact, the Ego becomes irrelevant.

So, the Ego will try, time and time again to regain control over us, its host. The Ego's most frequent tool in my experience is judgement. When the Ego realises that it can't get a hold of you regarding your judgement of yourself (because you've transcended judgement of yourself) it will find others to throw judgement against you. It will manipulate their Egos so that their Egos go on the attack as well.

I believe the path towards evolutionary growth and spiritual enlightenment is about choosing what Love would do, about choosing constructs of Love, about choosing compassion, about choosing honesty - in all cases, in all events, in all environments.

We don't know what is going on for the person across the path from us: the person who is attacking us, or yelling at us, or judging us. We don't know, but judgement is only ever adding the same energy to it that created it. We are adding Fear-based energy to a situation. You know what happens? It makes that Fear-based energy increase. It makes it more powerful and more influential into everyone's life.

We need to stop judging. We need to stop judging because when you stop judging, when you actually transcend the need to judge others or to complain about things that are going on, your

ENDING YOUR UNCONSCIOUSNESS

life will fundamentally change for the better. Your life will turn around, and you have no idea how magnificent your life can be until you have transcended judgement.

We need to move on from that. Judgement is what causes diplomatic wars. Judgement is what causes civil wars. Judgement is what causes division and destruction and separation. Judgement is not working for us. Judgement is a complete waste of your time and energy.

On any given day, I already feel like I don't have enough time to do the things that I want to do. If I'm wasting my time on judging people then I might as well be sitting there staring at my phone, playing silly games, as both are unproductive. Judgement is not helping others - and it certainly does not help me move forward in the Love-constructed life that I choose to develop and create.

Complaining about things won't fix them.

It will only make them worse.

The only thing that will fix them is to offer Love to what is happening. This is most easily done if we can start seeing the opportunity, the beauty, in everything we come across. Darkness cannot survive in the presence of Light. Fear-based constructs like judgement, criticism and complaining cannot survive in the presence of Love-based constructs.

CHAPTER SEVEN

So, if you're finding the need to judge, first we need to Recognise what is happening when that judgement arises within us. If we're feeling the need to complain, we must Recognise what is happening within us. Then we need to Reflect on what is going on, so we can choose what we want in return. When we're feeling the need to judge, we need to understand. We need to forgive ourselves. We need to Recognise our Ego at play and say "Thank you, Ego, but I don't believe what you are saying, and I don't need your help today. Good-bye."

It's just a very simple mantra of Recognising the Ego when it's at play and saying to the Ego, "I'm not interested in your lies." Moving away from judgement gives us more time to take action on Love based-constructs.

You'll be surprised at how many people I talk to about judgement. I tell them to analyse it throughout a week and keep a diary. They come back with pages and pages and pages of notes about what they were judging and when. In fact, they've stopped writing because they've suddenly started to realise that judgement is constant.

Women judge women for how they dress, their body shape, how they do their hair and whether they have makeup on for the day. Men judge men for their size and their demeanour and their arrogance. Women judge men, men judge women. We judge our

ENDING YOUR UNCONSCIOUSNESS

family and our friends. We all judge each other. It is part of everyday life nowadays, and it needs to stop.

If you want to choose a life of abundance; if you want to choose a life of joy and happiness and peace; if you want to build and design and create your life based on Love constructs; the first thing you need to do is get rid of judgement in your life. Recognise when it arises. Choose a Love-based construct instead. Take action on that Love-based construct. Offer judgement, offer the event, the situation and the life experience Love - because we are all here to experience everything that life has to offer.

Life has to offer both Love and Fear, but we don't need to suffer from it.

Chapter Eight

Forgive Yourself and Set Yourself Free

Harbouring ill thoughts about someone is poisoning you. Harbouring ill thoughts about yourself is poisoning you even further. It is poisoning you both psychologically and physically. Everything that we think about in a negative context creates a level of stress in the body which develops a range of toxins in the body. Your judgement of others is poisoning you.

We need to forgive.

I believe, first, we need to forgive ourselves. The vast majority of us live in a world where judgement is rife, and we fail

ENDING YOUR UNCONSCIOUSNESS

to take responsibility for everything that is going on in our life. We fail to see that we are the creators of our own life experience and that everything that is going on around us isn't necessarily a reflection of ourselves. However, our reaction to it is.

What we need to think about is forgiveness. We need to think about forgiving ourselves for not doing the right thing by ourselves. It's not just about judging ourselves for being fat, or judging ourselves for not looking handsome, or judging ourselves or others for not being nice people.

Some people judge themselves for not doing the right thing when they had the opportunity. Some people judge themselves for the sexual abuse that they experienced as a child. Some people judge themselves for the attacks that people inflict on them.

What people are doing is not a reflection of you. What people are doing is a reflection of them. How you react to that is a reflection of you.

Forgiving yourself will set you free. Freedom - honest, emotional, psychological and physical freedom from our stresses and our worries and our fears - comes from self-forgiveness. Forgiving others can also give you freedom as well, because you free yourself of the poisons that are created through judgement and complaining. You can also free them of your judgement. You release yourself of the burden of carrying the weight of others'

CHAPTER EIGHT

judgements.

Sometimes when I talk to people, either in my events or on a one-on-one basis, and I explain to them that they really need to forgive the other person, their first reaction is, "Why do I need to forgive somebody? They have done something wrong to me." What I'm saying is that you don't necessarily need to go and knock on the door and speak to them face-to-face and forgive them to their face. Yes, I believe that actually has a stronger benefit for both people involved, provided they are able to connect through the conversation. However, you can forgive them in yourself. Forgive them and forgive yourself for allowing them to have gotten to you, for allowing them to have troubled your mind, for allowing them to have taken up so much of your time.

Not everybody has that ability in their minds, because they're so caught up in their egoic Monkey Mind that they don't have the ability to be nice all the time. Not everybody is going to like you. That is a simple fact of life. What we can't do is run around and take responsibility for other people's actions. We can't run around and take responsibility for the judgement that comes in our direction. We can only take responsibility for our own thoughts, feelings, and actions. Sometimes we feel guilty about what we are doing. We made a mistake when we were a

ENDING YOUR UNCONSCIOUSNESS

teenager, or we made a mistake when we were a child. We judge ourselves for the things we have done and the choices that we have undertaken as adults.

We need to forgive ourselves. Life is about choice. Life is about learning. Life is about making (perhaps) the wrong choice and learning from that experience.

Successful people the world over know that there is no such thing as failure. There is only a set of actions that lead to a set of results. Sometimes those results are what we wanted, or what we desired, or what we expected. Other times, they are not. There is no failure in the sense of the word. There are only results. I believe the only way a failure can occur, or a mistake can occur, is if we choose not to learn from the experiences that are put before us. Rather, we must choose to learn and grow and personally develop from what is happening around us.

Forgiveness is the key.

Forgiveness of ourselves is the start. Forgiveness of those who cross us, those who try to harm us, those who try to attack us. Now, this isn't a new concept. This is not something I've made up, or I've created or invented. This has been around for millennia and for very good reason. Mostly because we aren't listening to the lessons here. Forgiveness is the key to all happiness.

CHAPTER EIGHT

Most of the troubles that we have in our lives, most of the heartache we experience, is completely and utterly made up by our own mind. It is our Ego running rampant, our Ego controlling us in every possible aspect. Until we start Recognising when the Ego comes up, and until we start making the choice to choose Love constructs like forgiveness, while transcending Fear based-constructs like judgement, guilt and shame, transcending the Ego is going to be very difficult to do.

You see, the Ego wants to control you. The Ego sits on your shoulder like a parrot constantly trash-talking in your ear. If it's not trash-talking to you, it's putting thoughts in your head that are trash-talking everybody else. Either way, judgement is not helping you. You are spending all of this time and energy on this negative Fear-based construct when you could be choosing to spend that energy on a Love-based construct. Transcending fear, transcending judgement, moving on and choosing to love people for the choices that they make, choosing to love people for the beliefs that they have, choosing to love people for the life they are choosing to create. Yes, it's not your life. Yes, you wouldn't do it that way. You wouldn't dress that way. You wouldn't look that way. You wouldn't drive a car that way. Yes, I get all of that, but there's not any reason to judge it. People have a right to make those choices. As do you.

ENDING YOUR UNCONSCIOUSNESS

Now, I have a rule that I don't believe people have a right to do something that harms another. However, I'm not their policeman. I'm not their judge, jury, and executioner, and neither should you be. If someone is harming someone that you love dearly, then stand up for them and get in the way and be brave, and be a hero. Protect them. But judgement in itself is not working, and will not help the situation one bit. Instead of judging someone for what they're doing, we need to offer that situation Love. We need to choose to love people for the choices that they make even though those choices are not our own choices. Even if those choices are not the type of choices we would make; even if those choices look to be an obvious mistake or will lead them to failure. We need to offer Love to that situation, not Judgement. We need to offer forgiveness to people because anything else is judgement, and that isn't working for us.

Love is compassionate. Love is joyful. Love is peaceful. Love would find a way to approach and to talk to them and to show them that perhaps there is an alternative path that would arrive at a better outcome for them. Love is gentle, and it whispers; our Ego is loud and boisterous and arrogant, because the Ego knows that if it is loud and if it stays loud in your head, you can't listen to your love-based inspiration.

We only experience things based on our past's reflection of

CHAPTER EIGHT

our future. This is why we have difficulty seeing everybody else's trials and torments, why we have difficulty seeing everybody else's troubles. We don't know what battles they have going on behind them because those battles are a result of the egoic mind in their lives being active as a result of their past experience. Now, at any point in time, we can hit the reset button and change that life experience. We can change a negative past life experience to a positive life experience. It is just a simple choice. We can all make that choice at any moment, and that choice needs to be based on Love. That choice needs to be based on Love-based constructs. But what I believe we shouldn't do is judge those that don't know any different.

We need to offer those Love-based constructs through taking action. We need to Reflect on what is happening that we don't want through Recognising it. Then, Reflect on what it is we do want by choosing a Love-based construct. Finally, take action on it to Resolve what is going on within us.

Forgiving ourselves is that resolution. Forgiving ourselves is the action that we need to take. For years I felt shame and guilt for some of the choices that I made as a kid, for some of the things that happened to me as a child. I lived with that shame and guilt for 20 years. It wasn't until I chose to forgive myself, and chose to forgive those who crossed me, those who judged me,

ENDING YOUR UNCONSCIOUSNESS

those who attacked me, that I had true freedom in my heart.

Now, this is something that all of you can do. Every person on this planet can do this. We just need to make a choice. It is a simple choice and we all can do it. Sometimes, though, we need to Recognise that a choice is even available to us. First, we need to know the impact that our judgement causes in our lives. Then we need to forgive ourselves so that we can move past the guilt and shame that has built up within us.

We need to transcend this so that we can move forward to leave the past behind and step into the present. It is there, in the present, where everything is possible.

It is never possible in the past, as it has already happened. It is never in the future, because that is always later. It can only ever happen in the Now. So Now is the time to stop your judgement, forgive yourself and others for everything that has ever happened in the past, and move forward, free of judgement, free of guilt and shame, and free of the limitations that the Fear-driven Ego inflicts on your life experience.

You deserve freedom, and it can only truly come from conscious, connected forgiveness.

Chapter Nine

Fear is An Illusion

One of the biggest misconceptions we have created as a collective unconscious society is that the boundaries and limitations we see in our lives - what holds us back and stops us from moving forward - are real. In fact, we have created so many boundaries in life that it honestly surprises me how we achieve anything at all. The irony is that each and every one of these boundaries are just a figment of our mind-based rhetoric. An illusion, if you will; a fabrication to help us feel more secure, to explain why we cannot do something, an excuse, or a story we tell to ourselves or to others.

We all do it. We have all done it for the majority of our lives. The biggest difference between us and truly successful people is that they do it a lot less often. They are not entirely free of the

ENDING YOUR UNCONSCIOUSNESS

illusion of boundaries, but they are better practiced at seeing them for what they are, and they have an entirely different set of boundaries compared to the rest of us. The reason why boundaries exist to some extent in all of us is because the Ego is present in all of us, and boundaries and limitations are a creation of the Fear-driven Ego and how it operates through our mind.

The Ego creates boundaries and limitations to control us, to restrict our success and our potential. The Ego knows that its path towards relevance and control over it's host (us) is infinitely more difficult when we are succeeding, reaching our potential, helping others succeed and better still, living in a consciously Love-driven life. The big challenge is that as life goes on we move past our first few knocks in our late teens and early twenties and start to develop an extensive library of "cannot do's" and "aren't able's" as we get older. If you are in your late forties to early fifties, you have a thousand and one more excuses and reasons why *not* to do anything than you have *to* do it. This is extremely common, and it is the real reason why people cannot achieve what is in their hearts, and why they cannot find abundance and prosperity in their lives. Quite simply, they either genuinely believe they don't have what it takes to do it, or they cannot do what is required to obtain it. They have too many years of built-up boundaries, limitations, and unhealthy beliefs working in

CHAPTER NINE

their daily lives. Have no fear though - because, although changing that mindset isn't all that easy, it is certainly possible with commitment and with a desire to see what is on the other side.

This was ultimately what was driving me. I wanted to see what was on the other side of Fear. Real, terrifying, stomach emptying, Fear. This type of Fear, to me, was representative of the ultimate battle between my mind and my desire to live. It was representative of the boundaries we create in our past experience of life, and how they influence our present day. When I started to explore my boundaries, I started to see a familiar pattern. The pattern was driven by the one common boundary-creating mechanism: my Beliefs.

There they were again. But they changed. Albeit unconsciously, I started to realise I had been changing my beliefs all my life. Some stayed very much the same - like my belief that we shouldn't harm others and that our choices in our own life shouldn't impact on the lives of others. Other beliefs were more fluid - like my sometimes-weekly changing beliefs moving from, "Alcohol is a highly addictive poison that controls my life experience," to "It's O.K., a couple of drinks won't do me any harm." As only an Alcoholic can understand, the madness of these changing beliefs is self-destructive.

ENDING YOUR UNCONSCIOUSNESS

My belief that snakes aren't here to harm me was, for a very long time, very different to my belief that spiders are terrifying, creepy-crawly demons from some inner hell-based damnation. Even that belief changed somehow (and certainly unconsciously) when I first decided one day to pick up some big hairy huntsman spider from the kids' bedroom and quietly walk him outside. Our boundaries are created within our mind, based on our beliefs, and are often heavily influenced by the Ego.

Now, although I had theorised by this stage that boundaries are just an illusion, I was aware of the Ego's influence in my day-to-day life experience, which helped me isolate the possibility that boundaries are just an Egoic, fictitious lie to keep us from truly understanding our inner potential. This in turn gave me a little bit of confidence to explore the matter further, despite the fact that the method of exploration I had decided on terrified me.

Most people would have gone to a theme park and ridden in a fast and scary roller-coaster or caught an elevator to the top floor of a very high building and leaned against the glass of one of its half-inch thick floor-to-ceiling windows, held on by industrial- strength silicone adhesive. But not me. That wasn't terrifying enough.

I needed something that the vast majority of the population would relate to as absolutely terrifying. I needed something that

CHAPTER NINE

everyone would see as a completely, ridiculously, stupid thing for a slightly overweight, forty-something desk jockey to do. Funnily enough, Michelle and my family thought I was going through another mid-life crisis. I reassured them that it was the still the same mid-life crisis I have been going through for years now, and I honestly was perpetuating it for as long as feasibly possible. The fact is, I am thoroughly enjoying my mid-life crisis, and I intend to keep doing so.

All jokes aside though, I wanted to do something that not only had meaning to me but could also be related to by most readers as a seriously extreme, boundary-pushing exercise. So, I decided that I would learn to skydive.

I want to be clear. This is no ordinary tandem skydive, where you are strapped onto another highly-experienced person and they jump out on your behalf and pull the chute and steer you down to earth. I wanted to do this solo. Jump out myself, pull my own chute, and steer myself to my obvious and apparently certain death. Again, what was I thinking?

So, I booked myself in, several months in advance, thinking at the time it was far enough off that I could easily back out. Little did I know that I would be very busy in the first quarter of this year, and so the time passed too quickly for me to come to my senses. I had organised to take the week off work not only to do a

ENDING YOUR UNCONSCIOUSNESS

single solo jump, but I booked in to do fifteen jumps within seven days to become a licenced skydiver. This way I figured I could fully explore the fear cycle, the process of coming out the other end, and carefully analyse my physiological and psychological responses. Then D-Day arrived.

It was Monday, on a cool and slightly overcast Autumn day in April. I was lucky because I had a professionally managed and fully equipped jump site only ten minutes from where I lived. The guys and gals who trained me and helped me through the process are a remarkably gentle bunch of souls, mellow and considerate with everyone that came through the doors. I love it when a local, coastal-town small business punches so far above their weight class and shows up all the big city competitors. I sincerely admire them greatly.

Monday was theory day: a day to get our heads around what was going to happen, what we needed to do. Most importantly, they ran us through every emergency scenario I could think of, and then some. It was a long day, and an unusual one for me. For the first time in a very long time I started to notice, as my anxiety rose, that the Fear process had begun. I knew on Monday that I was jumping first thing the next morning, early Tuesday morning. I had started to accept the reality of my situation. I went home Monday evening exhausted and terrified. I had no

CHAPTER NINE

real idea what was to come.

The sun rose the next day. Not that I could have known, because it was overcast, and the low clouds were sitting somewhere just above 7,000 feet. I hadn't really thought about the consequences of jumping in cloud cover because my mind was running at a million miles an hour. My heart rate was up a little, as were my excitement levels. Today had finally arrived, and my God, I hoped my affairs were in order.

I arrived at the jump site after a good night's sleep in my own bed, and everyone was fired up. We ran through a few simple procedures to refresh the mind, and we put on our jumpsuits. Pack on, altimeter, helmet, goggles, check. One last run through of the emergency procedures. Just in case my first chute doesn't open, I do have a second, emergency chute. I later realised that is little comfort when plummeting towards earth at terminal velocity. If the Fear process wasn't in full swing when I first got up in the morning, it sure as hell was now. Heart rate up, and I could feel it pounding in my chest. I could hear my heartbeat in my ears and I was having trouble listening to the pre-flight landing sequence. All I could focus on was that I was about to climb onto the wing strut of a small 185 Cessna light aircraft with no seats and a small exit door at 12,000 feet. Again, the illusion of safety.

ENDING YOUR UNCONSCIOUSNESS

We climbed into the plane in the reverse order of our exit, and the terror started to become real. I am sure my cool, steely exterior wasn't fooling anyone. I was terrified. The plane took off and climbed surprisingly fast, but not fast enough to stop my mind from getting into my headspace. I looked out of the window to enjoy the view, as if to distract myself for a few minutes until the clouds got in the way. I focussed on my breathing, noticed my thoughts going from one extreme to another, and then noticed my altimeter was telling me we were at approximately 8,000 feet. Exit was at 12,000 feet.

For the last 4,000 feet, I travelled in slow motion. My heart rate got louder, my head filled with panic, and then the red light came on signalling three minutes till jump time. I would like to say that the earth felt a long way down, but we were still in cloud cover and I had no idea if my altimeter was even remotely telling me the truth. This is where I thought of the importance of Faith. I knew I wasn't put on this earth to be a headline news story of a jump gone wrong. I knew my two instructors jumping with me to keep me on task had 12,000 and 9,000 jumps under their belts. A small calm came over me; not enough to slow my heart rate down, but enough to get me back to my thoughts, and the exit process, starting with goggles on, helmet on, radio on, and pre-jump checks. I remembered the exit routine, practiced on the

CHAPTER NINE

ground for what felt like a hundred times. I now knew why. Green light on. Door opening. Oh my God, please help me.

The first instructor stepped out onto the exit peg, hanging for dear life from the wing strut, making it look easy while hanging out over 12,000 feet of nothing but a hard and sudden stop. My turn. It is truly amazing how perspective works. That foot-long and inch-thick peg for my instructor's foot, and both of my feet, seemed big enough while practicing on the ground. Suddenly it didn't seem big enough anymore. Left hand out to grab the cold and icy wing strut. Right foot out on the peg. I am feeling how cold it is out here and feeling small icy bits stinging my cheeks. Right hand out, left foot, too. I lean forward with my left foot on the peg and my chest over the wing strut. So far so good.

With the cold wind biting my cheeks and a prop wind speed of 100 knots, I could feel the power of my predicament. My heart couldn't be heard. My adrenaline had stabilised on overdrive. Focussing on the exit procedure was important not only for safety reasons, but also to keeping the mind clear and panic free. I didn't realise at the time, but the adrenaline response actually creates the focus on the moment, a presence that is unique to adrenaline junkies, one that brings us back to the pinpoint of the here and now. It is beautiful, and it comes with a high that is

ENDING YOUR UNCONSCIOUSNESS

quite addictive, even if at first, born from terror.

I turn my head to the right to check in with the first instructor. He gives me the O.K. Head to the left to check in with the second instructor. She gives me the O.K. So, let's do this. Push up, one. Push down, two. Push off... Oh my!

It is at this point where you first realise that you are not attached to anything firm. You may be aware enough of each instructor holding your arms and legs to keep you stable while you get your head around what is happening, but it doesn't stop you from kicking your legs and waving your arms like you are free-falling to your death. This may have something to do with the obvious reality of your current situation.

Soon this feeling passes as you stabilise in the air. Arms and legs out, back arched, head up, you find it more difficult to breath than normal because of the rushing air. The noise of the air rush is akin to sticking your head out of a car window at 200 kilometres an hour, until you realise there is no car and you are still 10,000 feet up and approximately sixty seconds to a very quick death.

Then the processes kick in with a gentle shake from the instructor. Check pull cord. I reach back with my right had to show that I can find my pull cord. Done. Check again. Now check altimeter. 8,000 feet and falling fast. Stabilise, check arch of

CHAPTER NINE

back and position of hands. Check altimeter again. 6,000 feet. Prepare to pull cord. Watching altimeter for 5,500 feet. Check.

I wave off both instructors with both hands, reach back for pull cord, grab and quickly pull and throw. This is the point, if you haven't done so before, were you finally realise your mortality. You start counting to six as per your deployment process. You feel the chute pull out of your pack with a jolt. You go from a horizontal, arms and legs out position to vertical in an instant as you feel your chute open and fill. You look up in a panic to check it has filled while still counting to six. You count to six because it can take up to six seconds to release and deploy your chute to a full fill, and again I later realised it is also to give you something to focus on, so you don't jump to premature conclusions that your chute hasn't opened properly.

This point was an incredibly emotional point for me - and not only because you suddenly realise how eternally grateful you are for your chute opening properly. I went from adrenaline-filled noise to quiet relief in a matter of seconds. I realised I was no longer falling but flying. I felt free, peaceful, high as a kite, and most importantly, safe. My emotions quickly rose up within me, like a wave from my dangling legs, up through my chest and into my head. A huge emotional cry bursts out without notice. This is the moment when you are at your most authentic self. You no

ENDING YOUR UNCONSCIOUSNESS

longer have any aspect of physical world unconsciousness, as you cry heartily and uncontrollably. Immense relief washes over you as you realise your accomplishment, and you are relieved to know you not only survived, but wow, you nailed it. Your nose runs, your eyes spill over and you feel like you have never felt before. Every bit of tension, every worry, stressful moment and care you ever had in the world is now out, flying with the birds, free and never to be known again. You experience a moment of clarity, you feel connected to everything for the first time, and your immortality is as obvious to you now as your mortality was a few seconds before.

Life feels so important all of a sudden. Everything I held dear to my heart I wanted to embrace in an instant. This is what happens on the other side of Fear. This space, this moment, has no Ego - none at all. Only pure, unadulterated, unconditional Love.

The crackle of the one-way radio in my ear brings me back to reality, as I realised I still have to land this beast. My instructors are already landing, and I have to check that my controls work. Flare once (as I pull down on the two toggles to lower the back of the chute, which slows your forward speed down dramatically). Flare twice. Thank God for that. It works.

I start remembering the pre-flight landing sequence I

CHAPTER NINE

couldn't hear earlier because my stomach was pushing for a fast exit out of my throat and arse, simultaneously. I look for the windsock, checking wind direction, and I decide to play with levers that control my chute. A few turns here, and a few turns there. I don't want to do too much, because I'm worried about breaking it and ruining what has been a great (yet terrifying) time up until now.

The perspective of speed and the ground rapidly approaching takes a few jumps to master, so they have a third instructor giving me instructions via the radio in my ear to ensure a safe and happy landing. I move across wind, and then into the wind for final descent. I half flare my chute, and then full flare because I'm coming in too fast. The chute slows me down rapidly, to a slow walk and then a gentle stop. At this point I realise I have lifted my legs despite being able touch the ground and I gently land on my arse with a bump.

Emotions rise again. It burst out of me. I did it. I am safe. I am completely O.K. I sit and cry uncontrollably for a moment. The radio instructor knows what's going on. He has seen it a thousand times. He respects my space and need to unload, and gives me a moment to get myself together. I appreciate it.

I think about this moment for what seems like months. I process it as I did my jumps after that. Each jump became easier

ENDING YOUR UNCONSCIOUSNESS

until I replaced fear with excitement. It becomes apparent to me that the fear-based adrenaline response is very similar to the excitement. But it just feels so much yummier. It truly is delicious.

The reason why I encourage people at any point in time to first of all, Recognise what their Fear is, Reflect on possible alternatives to the Fear-based experience that they really want to experience, and then Resolve it through taking action on it, is because the process in itself helps us stay present.

The action in regard to proving that your Fears don't exist and that they are just an illusion, is to do what you're afraid of. For me, I'd always experienced a Fear of heights. The Fear of heights when you're at 12,000 feet, or later on in your jumping process when you're at 15,000 feet, is a very present experience indeed. That's pretty high up in the air!

It is fascinating how Fear runs through your mind. That is ultimately your highly-trained and well-practiced, Fear-driven Life Experience: your perception of life which has been trained over a very long period of time by society, by your parents, by all these other people who say you can't do this and you can't do that. The whole "helicopter parenting" nowadays is definitely part of that process. We overly protect our kids against normal everyday life experience moments because of our own egoic-

CHAPTER NINE

limiting thoughts.

This training for Fear happens with the Ego in your head and it is constant from an early age. The older we get without understanding the way the Ego operates and the way it interacts with our Life Experience, the more trained we are in that approach, and you'll notice this in a lot of people who don't stop to actually try and understand their Life Experience. They don't stop to understand Love, Fear and the way the Ego operates, and they begin to doubt themselves about some very simple things - things that in their twenties and thirties they could do quite easily, like starting a new job, furthering their education, and going back to study.

They fail to see the fact that nothing has changed, except that they are more capable and a little bit wiser and more experienced than they were when they were younger. The Ego has us believing that we can't do this or that, that we are not smart enough, or that we don't have enough time or money, or we need this, and we need that before we can do anything - and it's all an illusion. It's all a complete fabrication. It's an absolute lie created by the egoic mind.

It's really interesting when you find a Fear - and it doesn't have to be anything particularly big. It might be swimming in the ocean, a fear of heights, standing on the edge of a cliff, or

ENDING YOUR UNCONSCIOUSNESS

hopping on a motorbike with an experienced rider giving you a lift. For some people, catching a bus is scary, starting a new job is scary, going to social events where you don't know anybody is scary.

These examples can be little things that we can face and prove to ourselves that we can do them - to prove to ourselves that the egoic voice that we've been hearing in our head is telling us a lie and is trying to get us to believe something that simply doesn't exist: Boundaries and Limitations.

Think about your Fears. Recognise your Fears. Reflect on those Fears and determine what it is you want instead. For me, I wanted to do something a little bit crazy. I wanted to do something really energetic. I wanted to jump out of a plane and do something adrenaline-filled and exciting because for me (and I was well into my early forties when I did that) I actually wanted to prove to myself that I could do something new and exciting and something very, very different. I also wanted to show my boys (who were coming into early teenage years at the time) that as you get older, you don't need to stop living life. You don't need to stop doing new things. I wanted to show them that whatever you set your mind to you can do. Nothing should let that egoic, Fear-driven mind get control of your Life Experience and stop you from appreciating life and everything that it has to offer.

CHAPTER NINE

Once I understood that my mind is not the master of my experience, that the Ego can only speak in a language of lies, and that I am the creator of my life experience, a certain clarity rose over me. A peacefulness that can only come from the new-found belief that the boundaries that I have always believed were real are just an illusion - a complete fabrication of the mind. Fear is simply an illusion created by the mind.

I have tested this out many times, with everything I can muster, across multiple aspects of my life, my work and my relationships. I have tested this through many others to create the same results. We have yet to find real tangible boundaries because they are all created by the mind-based Ego, a Fear-driven Ego that fights for its own relevance, one that cannot tell the truth.

This all starts with understanding that we are not the thoughts in our head. We are the calm awareness listening to those thoughts. The Soul within us *is* us. The one true "us." Listening to the minds Fear-driven diatribe is counterproductive to everything we intuitively desire. Next, we must understand that we are the only ones that can create our life experience. We can create it through the Fear-driven Egoic mind, or we can create it with the same foundation of which everything in life is created: through Love.

ENDING YOUR UNCONSCIOUSNESS

You are your Soul. Not your body. Not your mind, and certainly not your ego. You can do whatever you set your desires to. Size and scale are no boundary for the universe, for you, for your soul, or for all the beings that help you on your path. If you want a life of riches, abundance, selfless service to others, or all of the above, it is only your choice away.

Only you can create your life. I decided to create a life without boundaries. Without restrictions. A limitless life for me and for everyone I can share it with. This belief gives us a creative freedom that we have never experienced. And I promise you, it is truly beautiful - and completely yours to create, too.

Chapter Ten

We Always Have a Choice

Most people that I speak to genuinely believe that they no longer have a choice about how their day-to-day life happens. We build our lives in such a way that we end up with big mortgages and car payments, we have children to feed, and therefore we've got to have a job that pays us on a weekly or fortnightly basis. We need that regular income coming in. We need the security from our job, and we start to feel like we no longer have a choice about the way our life manifests. We get up every morning, work all day and head home at the end of the day. Some of us spend hours in traffic - again, something we don't think we have a choice about.

You do have choices. You don't have to purchase the nice house, in the nice area. You don't. I never said there weren't

ENDING YOUR UNCONSCIOUSNESS

consequences to your choices. But the consequences don't ever remove the choice you actually do have. The choice is always there.

What I want to talk about is the fact that you do have a choice. The choice is yours, and you can make a decision at any time to change it or to accept it. In fact, most days, you are choosing to get up get out of bed, get yourself organised, hop into the car, drive for an hour to work, sit in the office for eight hours, then drive home and repeat, rinse and recycle every single day for the rest of the year (or what feels like the rest of your life). You are choosing misery and a life unfulfilled.

Now, the thing about choice is that it is very real. You can, at any point, choose to change the metrics in your life that create this experience of lack of choice, into a life or an experience of an abundance of choice. I once thought that I didn't have a choice until I woke up and realised that the life that was making me unhappy was merely the consequence of my choices. Perhaps not great choices, but my choices nonetheless.

So, I decided to do something about it, and I did what any sane person would do in such a dilemma. I bought a farm. I chose to no longer do the nine to five. I no longer wanted to experience that day-to-day suffering, so I decided that I wanted to go and operate a farm. It wasn't without its sacrifices, and certainly not

CHAPTER TEN

without its consequences, but at least I was making choices that were right for me for a change.

Now, with every choice comes a consequence. That is unavoidable. It is the way the Universe works. You cannot make a choice without consequences appearing, and those consequences are either good or bad. Any consequence is a direct relation to the choice that we make. If we need to change the consequence, we need to change the choice. So, if I no longer want to be doing the nine to five slog every single day that is making me unhappy (and probably also impacting my health), I need to start making proactive and positive choices that change that result. If I am living a life that is unfulfilling, I need to make a set of different choices to the ones I am already making.

However, sometimes we need to sit back and think about what process we may want to use to evaluate the choice. I use my Recognise, Reflect and Resolve technique over and over again for a range of different applications because it is so simple and effective. It forces me to better understand what is happening in my Life Experience. We need to Recognise what's happening in our Life Experience before we can Reflect on what we desire as an alternative; only then can we determine what action we need to take to Resolve it.

So, when we're thinking about choice, we need to think

ENDING YOUR UNCONSCIOUSNESS

about what is happening within our Life Experience that we don't like. Do we not like the job because it's boring and soulless? Do we not like it because the people we work with are really unhappy, or maybe they're just not very nice? Do we not like it because of its location, or do we not like it because it is not something that remotely interests us? These are all very different reasons that may require very different choices. You see, by Recognising what is not working for us we can actually start to identify other opportunities, alternatives that may work for us. But if we fail to Recognise it properly, how could we possibly fix it effectively?

Most people think that they don't have the courage, the bravery, the money or the opportunity to be able to make the changes in their life that they truly desire. I am here to tell you that you do. In fact, you are the only one who does.

You create your Life Experience. You are the only being in the Universe that can create your Life Experience. Nobody else can do it for you. Yes, it is easy to get caught up in the egoic, Fear-driven pity party or blame others or outside influences for your situation, but only you are to blame for the experience of an unhappy life. Blaming others or outside influences - well, that's just the Ego talking to you, trying to stop you from taking responsibility. The Ego doesn't want you to be happy, because

CHAPTER TEN

when you're happy, you're not connected to its Fear-based consciousness. The Ego doesn't want you to be successful, because when you're successful, you're happy.

The Ego doesn't want you connecting with other people. It doesn't want you living your dream, or doing what you really desire in life, because by doing all of those things, you are living in a place of constructed Love. When you are doing those things the Ego is disconnected, irrelevant, and unable to control you or your Life Experience.

So, we need to think about what those choices are and how those choices are controlling us. We often make choices that end up controlling us. Sometimes we need to consider that some of the choices we made in an earlier belief system are no longer relevant choices that are healthy for us in a later belief system.

We develop beliefs over time. As a toddler, we learn a set of beliefs that are passed on to us from our parents, because that's who we look up to. Then, when we enter our teenage years, we start to change our belief system and base our beliefs on the values of our peers and the different people we look up to. When we leave home we change our beliefs again, and usually that's based on the people we work with and a new group of people we look up to. The problem is, sometimes we make choices, or we meet people that are right for that particular point in our life, but

ENDING YOUR UNCONSCIOUSNESS

as our life progresses and we change as a human being, other things change as well: the people around us, our relationships, what is right for us, and what is wrong for us. Sometimes we need to adapt and re-examine our choices over and over again to make sure that the choices we make are constantly healthy and moving us in a forward direction.

I think most of us are unhappy because those choices that we made when we were younger are still impacting our day-to-day life today; they don't actually fit or work or match what our current desires or given objectives are. But we are still trapped in this way of thinking that we still need to work this job because we have a mortgage to pay, or that we still need to live in this particular space, because the kids' school is around the corner. Sometimes we stay where we are because we have some friends that live locally, or we have family nearby and that family needs us.

What I'm trying to say is that when we start to properly examine our past choices we realise that those choices are a little more fluid than we think. We can change jobs. We can change where we live. The people around us, our children or our friends and family, will understand. In fact, there is every possibility that they will support the change that is necessary because they see that we need it.

CHAPTER TEN

The biggest cause of what we call our midlife crisis is that our past choices and past beliefs no longer serve the desire we have in hearts of what we want from life now. Those that don't understand see us as reactive, lashing out at life, making silly decisions like buying sports cars or farms. All that is happening is that, either consciously or unconsciously, we realize that we need to make a change because the last set of big choices we made are no longer making us happy or are the cause of us becoming unhappy.

The Universe puts opportunities in front of us. Sometimes those opportunities are driven by unhappiness with our Life Experience. That unhappiness gets greater and greater and greater until the pain that we are experiencing, at that point, is greater than the pain associated with the change of moving forward. This is the same as the situation we call "Rock Bottom." Our life experience becomes so desperate that we are forced to make a change. The problem then becomes: which choice do we make?

First, we need to look at the choices that we have made and figure out which ones are still working for us and which ones aren't. Then, we need to reflect on what alternative choices we can make that move us out of our pain and into more pleasure in our Life Experience.

ENDING YOUR UNCONSCIOUSNESS

So, if we're unhappy in our job, we need to Recognise why we are unhappy. If it is about the people, then a new job of the same type elsewhere may suffice. If it is about the type of work, going elsewhere and doing the same thing will not help. If you are unhappy about where you live, maybe you can move towns and move jobs altogether and completely start afresh. Even that process in itself can be invigorating and can give us a new opportunity to start over, hit the Reset Button, and create a new version of ourselves.

Recognising the choices we have is very important. We always have a choice, even when it appears that we don't. We've always had a choice and we always make choices. Even when we're not making a choice, we are still making a choice to not make a choice. Making choices is unavoidable. What we need to start doing is to make choices that lead us in the direction of the Life Experience we are choosing to create.

What we need to think about is: what are the intended consequences we want from the choices that we're making? And will the choice that we're thinking of making lead to those intended consequences? By understanding where we want to go in life we can then start mapping out what actions we need to take to help us resolve the issue that we are experiencing and move forward with a better, happier Life Experience.

CHAPTER TEN

Ask yourself, are you living your life the way you want to live it? Or is there something that you've always wanted to do, or a place you've always wanted to live? An occupation or an opportunity you've always wanted to take?

It is your choice to make. It is your opportunity to do what is required.

And only you can do it.

Chapter Eleven

Your Beliefs and Why You Need to Change Them

Our belief system is the foundation of everything we experience. We all have a belief system; it is unavoidable. This belief system, no matter what it is based upon, creates a set of rules that determine whether what we experience as life, in any given moment, is either pleasure or pain. If we are living an unhappy life of depression, anxiety or unfulfillment, it is because the belief system that we carry around with us no longer serves us. It is honestly that simple.

When we're born we develop a set of beliefs based on our parental influence. Our parents are all that we know, and they shape our entire world, from day one. As we start to enter our teenage years, we start experiencing our beliefs in a different way, which leads us to challenge our beliefs, often resulting in us shaping a new set of beliefs based less on our family life relationships and more from our peers and the people that we look up to.

When we arrive into early adulthood and we're thinking of leaving home, we start to change our belief systems again as we focus on the people we work with, our peers as well as the people we look up to, for inspiration or guidance. I've noticed over many years something interesting: that the vast majority of individuals in our greater society allow their beliefs to stagnate - to rot, so to speak - on the floor of our mind's compost heap.

Most people don't check in with their beliefs on a regular basis to determine if these beliefs are still working for them or holding them back. In fact, I think most people arrive at a breaking point, as they enter into their mid-forties or fifties, when they experience what we crudely refer to as their midlife crisis. This breaking point is like two tectonic plates under the ocean that are ready to spawn an earthquake. Pressure builds up over a period of time and then eventually something's got to give. The belief system that they'd carried for some twenty or thirty years hasn't been reworked and re-evaluated over time, and it no longer works for them. The pressure that builds up is created by

CHAPTER ELEVEN

the discord between what their belief system determines they should be experiencing compared to what they are actually experiencing. The belief system created in their late teens or early adult years is delivering them a negative Life Experience because it is out of date, not relevant, and simply wrong for them now.

The beliefs that we develop at different points in our life create a set of rules in our head that determine whether we are having a positive Life Experience or a negative Life Experience. The rules determine whether we feel pleasure or pain in any particular situation. For instance, if you have a particular rule that someone should call you on your birthday to wish you a happy birthday, and they don't, that will lead you to experiencing pain. But if that person gets on the phone and calls you, you feel pleasure. If you have a rule that when you tell someone you love them, that they should reciprocate and return the statement of love, and they do, you feel pleasure, you feel fabulous and wanted and perhaps even desired; but if they don't, you feel crushed, deserted and all alone.

Furthermore, if you have a rule where someone should buy you flowers on Valentine's Day, or that everybody should drive at the speed limit, or that people should treat you nicely and courteously when you're working in an office, and they don't fulfil those expectations, you will feel pain. When people are

ENDING YOUR UNCONSCIOUSNESS

failing to meet those rule expectations that you have in your head it effectively delivers pain into your experience, creating what we call a negative Life Experience. If they meet the parameters of your rules then you will experience pleasure, or a positive Life Experience.

Let's get one thing clear. This is not because of their actions. They are not causing the pain; in fact, they probably have no idea what the rules in your head are. Your belief, and the rule that is based on that belief, creates that pain. No one else is responsible for your life experience. Never. Only you, and your perception of what you are experiencing, creates your life experience - and depending on what your beliefs are, you will experience more pleasure or more pain in your life experience.

These belief-based rules are as unique as we are. We all have them, but they develop into a highly complex web of conditioning over a long period of time. They are based on our upbringing, cultural influences, environmental influences, and our desires and experiences in any given moment.

Have no Fear, because you can change your rules at any time. But it needs to be done properly, otherwise you can do more harm than good. Our Beliefs are at the top of the hierarchy, and they overrule any and all rules that are created below them. If you change the rule without evaluating the belief that creates it,

CHAPTER ELEVEN

the belief will overwhelm the new rule in the moment of each life experience that relates to it.

For instance, if you have a core belief that a successful relationship is born through both people having the same beliefs, you can imagine the challenges you are going to have here. Firstly, there is the pain that arises when your partner challenges your beliefs, or when their actions are contrary to the rules you have based upon those beliefs. If you then try to change the rule, to allow this behaviour, that rule will likely end up clashing with the core belief that created it originally, creating pain in your experience - despite them fulfilling the rule you later created. The problem is that you haven't evaluated and altered the belief that has made the rule. You have not addressed the base-level construct that is creating it all.

When we look at our Life Experience, and decide that we want to change it, we need to go back to our belief system, break it all down to its core constructs, and then rework, change or update the belief system to work within the parameters of what we are trying to create. This is no different to building a skyscraper upon the foundation of an aircraft hangar. An aircraft hangar was built with a very specific purpose in mind and with a shallow foundational structure. If we were to build a skyscraper on top of it, we couldn't just remove the building above the

ENDING YOUR UNCONSCIOUSNESS

ground and start adding sixty floors. We would need to pull everything apart, dig it all up and build the right foundation to safely hold those sixty floors. Building a new life is no different.

This isn't the easiest thing to do, because most of us cannot articulate what our beliefs are. This is why we need to run through the Recognise, Reflect and Resolve process to better analyse each belief and how it is working for us. These beliefs are part of everything we do; they give us pleasure or pain, they make us successful or unsuccessful. They are either our blockers or our enablers. It is essential to get it right, because everything flows from this one foundation. When I realized all of this, I started to rethink my entire belief system. Whenever I looked deeply into a belief I realized that it was not only out of date, but it was creating pain in my Life Experience because of the way they are all interconnected.

We all have different beliefs, because they are developed over a period of time based on our environment, our culture, our upbringing, our friends and the people we look up to. Our belief sets are as unique as we are. I would say nearly everybody on the planet has a different set of beliefs (or subsets of beliefs) to the people that are around them, despite also having a lot of commonality in our collective beliefs. This is not only common, it must be expected.

CHAPTER ELEVEN

This is why I cannot tell you what beliefs you must have to help you become successful. I can guide you, but it is always best determined in one-on-one sessions so that it can all be evaluated properly. It can take time, because we often don't become aware of what some beliefs are until we experience a situation that brings it into our conscious awareness.

Even people in long-term partnership arrangements (like marriage) often have different belief systems, despite the fact that they obviously interact and communicate in very similar environments. Even children, even twins or triplets, that grow up in the same house and the same schooling environment, develop different sets of beliefs.

Our beliefs are based on the past Life Experience that we have. They are based on our interactions with our parents, our peers, our siblings, the people we look up to, the people we idolise, the people we work with and the people we live with. Our beliefs ultimately change and morph over a long period of time. When we start to evaluate the fact that our beliefs aren't working for us then we see why we need to change them - because we are experiencing regular pain, or a regular negative Life Experience. Only through reassessing those beliefs can we start to change our life from a negative Life Experience to a positive Life Experience.

I went through a process a number of years ago where I

ENDING YOUR UNCONSCIOUSNESS

started to evaluate who I was, the environment that I was acting out in, and how my behaviours and my actions were coming out. I started to realise that my beliefs were letting me down because the rules I had in place were not the same rules that everybody else has. My beliefs were significantly out of date because they directly clashed with my newfound desires for peace, for joy and for happiness.

Now, I'm not saying you have to change your rules to what everybody else's rules are. That's not what this is about. You are a free-spirited, beautiful human being that can have the beliefs and thoughts that you so desire. What we need to understand is the rules that lead to our behaviours create consequences. Every choice, every thought, every feeling we have creates a consequence. Sometimes the consequences are great. Sometimes the consequences are not so great. Sometimes they're also a little bit indifferent, but most of the consequences are either good or bad in our experience.

Now, if we have a set of beliefs, and other people are not meeting those beliefs, but we haven't shared with them what our beliefs or our rules are for our Life Experience, we can't possibly blame them for not having met those beliefs. We can't possibly blame them for not meeting our expectations. Also, in my opinion, we need to respect their right to choose a different set of

CHAPTER ELEVEN

beliefs, whether they know or understand our beliefs or not.

I see this particularly in counselling a lot of couples, where you can see that there are two very different belief systems and two very different sets of rules associated with those belief systems. The first thing I try to do is to establish an understanding of what one person's belief system is relation to what the other person's belief system is, or what one person's rule is (given the circumstances) and what another person's rule is. The clarity this provides is incredible, because people realise that if their partner doesn't know what their rules are, they can't possibly be expected to meet them, now can they?

Most of the time, just through the process of sharing each other's rules, we can open up a dialogue associated with how we're interacting with people, how our actions are impacting their Life Experience, and how their actions are impacting ours. Often, just going through the process of that discussion helps empower people to share information so they can start to rectify their relationship issues. The clarity that comes from better understanding each other is incredible.

Sometimes, as part of that dialogue, we also start to evaluate that some of the rules we have are actually unhelpful or counterproductive to what we want. That is because they're out of date with what we desire our Life Experience to be. They might

ENDING YOUR UNCONSCIOUSNESS

have been suitable for us once upon a time. But in this new relationship that we have, it doesn't work that way. Or, we no longer want the consequences that come as a result of those rules, so we need to change the rule and the belief system those rules are based on.

Now, I'm not necessarily talking about changing your fundamental belief system. If you want to delve deeper into that type of model, that's absolutely fine. However, I'm talking about starting with simple beliefs. For instance, I have a belief that all people should treat each other with courtesy and respect and that we should not ever do anything or take action on anything that causes another person harm.

Now, despite having that belief system, I started to realise that my own actions and behaviours weren't following those rules. What I was doing was counteractive to other rules that I have. This type of conflict happens in our ruleset all the time, if we allow those rules to become out of date with our current desires.

What I was doing was either causing harm to other people or causing a problem for other people in their Life Experience because I had a certain set of rules that weren't being met. I started to re-evaluate my rules and realised that, instead of running around trying to change the entire world around me to

CHAPTER ELEVEN

suit me, it was easier (and more productive) to adapt my own rules to meet the environment around me. The benefit of doing that was that suddenly my Life Experience changed from being consistently negative in its overall approach to being highly positive.

My level of happiness went from something that might have been quite ordinary to quite high. Sometimes it is easier to sit down and just talk to someone and say, "This is what is happening to me, and this is why." Not only so they can understand, but so we can open up a dialogue to try and make things better.

Just because you believed something once doesn't mean you need to continue to believe it. We change, our environments change, and the people that we share our life with change; so I believe our belief structures also need to adapt to the ever-changing Life Experience. I think we need to check in with ourselves on a regular basis to determine whether our belief system is working for us or whether the rules that are based off of our belief system are creating positive Life Experiences for us, rather than negative Life Experiences.

We all deserve to be happy. It is a natural-born right. If we are living an unhappy life, it is because our belief system is no longer relevant, given our new life expectations. Changing our

ENDING YOUR UNCONSCIOUSNESS

belief system will fundamentally free us to live any life we so choose, a new life consisting of whatever success means to us, and whatever happiness means to us.

We are the only beings in the entire universe that can create our Life Experience, and it all starts from the foundation that is created by our beliefs.

Chapter Twelve

Your Uniqueness Will Lead You to Your Life Purpose

Everybody on this planet is different. But why do we always try to be the same? Why do we want to do the same jobs or perform the same roles as other people? Why dress the same, or do our hair the same? Why are we so keen to be what everybody else has already been? Why are we so keen to do what other people have already done?

We are all unique. We are all different, and for very good reason. We're raised differently. We have different parents, who were also raised differently. We come from different backgrounds, different jurisdictions, with different cultures. We go to different schools. We have different beliefs. We build different rules on those beliefs. We have different expectations.

ENDING YOUR UNCONSCIOUSNESS

We look differently. We act differently. So, why are we so desperate to be the same?

I say, embrace your uniqueness. Embrace the fact that you are different. Be excited about it. If all of us were skinny, and beautiful, and sexy, if we all thought the same, dressed the same, and believed the same things, wouldn't that be boring?

I love the fact that we have different religions. I love the fact that we believe different things. I love the fact that we dress differently and cook food differently. I love the fact that we have different thought processes. I love the fact that some of us are caught in our head and others are perhaps a little freer of the Ego. I love the fact that some of us struggle and some of us succeed, because that is what life is. That is Life as an expression of itself.

I want to talk to you about the fact that your uniqueness is the key to your personal success. Your uniqueness is the reason behind your chosen path. I believe that when we are in the spiritual world, in heaven (whatever your belief system is) we decide to reincarnate into this body, and we decided to live a certain life, a bit of a path.

Perhaps it's destiny. I don't know. But one thing I do believe is that we have chosen a particular path ahead of time. And when we arrive here, part of the deal is that we have chosen a particular set of parents; and, if we've already got siblings by that stage,

CHAPTER TWELVE

we've chosen those particular siblings too. And those parents and those siblings are the basis for getting us started on our path.

Our parents give us a certain set of characteristics, and coupled with our siblings, they give us a particular Life Experience, in our formative early days. I believe that that is all part of our choice before we incarnate. So, when we incarnate, the one rule about this whole physical world existence is that, over time, we forget why we're here (particularly after the first few years).

Then we end up on a slightly different path over time, with the idea that, hopefully, at some particular point, if we have lost our way, we can come back. There are numerous fables in all aspects of different religions that talk about this aspect. And I believe what it is all about is the need to embrace our uniqueness.

There are so many people out there in the world that are talking about their uniqueness, and how it was directly responsible for them being who they are now, and why they have achieved the level of success that they have.

I believe that, first of all, we need to accept the fact that we are unique. Accept the fact that we're not as handsome as someone else, or as pretty as someone else, or that we need to be something else. We don't need to be anyone but ourselves - the true representation of what we are, because of what we came here

ENDING YOUR UNCONSCIOUSNESS

to do. The point is that everyone is very, very different, and for very good reason.

The majority of people that come to me are unhappy in their life. Some of this has to do with the fact that their belief systems are out of date with their Life Experience, and they need to update them and reconnect with them - or recreate them. But a lot of these people are unhappy in their life because they don't know what they're here to do. They feel unfulfilled because they have lost sight of their purpose in life.

They've finally figured out that sitting behind a desk and doing the nine to five drum, spending an hour in the traffic in the morning and an hour in the traffic in the evening, only to come home to kids already asleep and a partner who's tired, is not actually living their life, and certainly not how they had planned when they were younger. They are unhappy with what they're doing, and they start to believe that there has to be something more to life.

Now, I quite clearly tell them, "There is something more. Absolutely there is something more." Life is not about the nine to five drum. We didn't come here to sit behind a desk and just be bored out of our brain every day. We came here to do something quite remarkable, and I think it is very, very important for us to embrace that and accept that idea.

CHAPTER TWELVE

The problem is that the majority of people don't know what that is. They don't know what it is for them. They don't know why they came here, why they incarnated into this life, into this body.

What was the purpose of their current Life Experience?

Now, sometimes, our purpose for this current Life Experience is to have a fairly normal life. I believe some people came here, very selflessly - not selfishly, but selflessly - to give to others. Sometimes parents come together to give life to a particular child, and without them coming together and doing so, that child's life, and the purpose that has great prospects for humanity, would have never existed. Sometimes that process can happen over a period of generations, where the universe conspires to make sure a certain set of things happen, to create the perfect environment for something that's really important to happen.

Sometimes life isn't that of a superhero. It isn't remarkable, it isn't the life of Jesus or Buddha or Mother Teresa or Tony Robbins or Eckhart Tolle or Wayne Dyer. But even if our life isn't that remarkable, our life is still integral to everything that happens. It's still absolutely, vitally important to what the next steps are. I believe we all have a purpose, and our purpose is as unique and as varied as we are as individuals. I believe it is our

ENDING YOUR UNCONSCIOUSNESS

job - the requirement of coming here and incarnating into this physical body - to fulfil that purpose. If we don't fulfil that purpose, we don't create an opportunity for another person to learn, to grow, to develop. Or, sometimes our opportunity, our purpose, is the dependency that their purpose relies on so that then they can move forward with their Life Experience.

We need to be the person that we are communicating to the world what we need to communicate. We need to do what we need to do. We need to help who we need to help. Then we can produce a flow-on effect, a ripple effect if you like, or a cascading effect. If the water doesn't fill up in the lake, it can't possibly overflow down the waterfall. And if it doesn't overflow down the waterfall, the animals and the creatures further downstream don't get the water that they need to survive.

Our purpose in life is actually very similar and I believe your uniqueness is directly related to finding out what your purpose is. If I hadn't experienced what I did as a teenager, I wouldn't be here now and talking to you. I know dozens of other people who say the same.

Every motivational speaker on the planet has had some level of tragedy in their life - or call it "rock-bottom" - that has snapped them out of their funky, negative mindset and got them to achieve remarkably great things in life. The way this all comes

CHAPTER TWELVE

together is about the way we were raised and the perspective that we gained from our upbringing. Now, whether that's an upbringing of just a couple of decades, or whether it's like me, four decades large and growing, that perspective fundamentally shapes who we are, making us even more unique than what we were twenty years ago. The older we get, and the more unique we become, I believe the more specific the relationship between that uniqueness and our chosen path of destiny (if you want to call it) becomes.

So, I say: if you're a little bit different, a little bit quirky, a little bit funky, a little bit weird, own it. Be proud of it. Live it and breathe it. If you're a geek or a nerd, I say bring it on. Be proud of that.

If you're an athlete and you're strong and powerful, or you're a model and you're particularly gorgeous, I say own that too - because all of that is part of the uniqueness that is part of our journey on this earth. We need to find why we're here.

I believe that is ultimately what our purpose is: to remember why we're here, something that we forgot somewhere around the age of three or four, which is usually when nightmares start to happen in children. I actually think that they're part and parcel of them suddenly starting to realise that they are in this physical body, this physical environment, and they've forgotten about the

ENDING YOUR UNCONSCIOUSNESS

spiritual world; they're starting to forget about what their path is, and they don't want to, because they've actually got a job to do.

But they're still not capable and knowledgeable enough in the physical world context, in this physical world body, to be able to get on and do it. It all may be rudimentary at this point because they are not physically mature enough to deliver on their path, but their connection to it is no less meaningful. Some children have longer-term memories than that, remembering past Life Experiences which are verifiable.

Some people don't discover what their true path is except through great tragedy in their life, this rock-bottom experience. Some people seek opportunity, but they're too caught up in their Ego monkey-mind to be able to see the opportunity when the Universe presents it.

This is all O.K., because this is all part of the journey. Sometimes when we stop and relax enough to actually start to take on board our inspiration and to listen to what our heart is trying to tell us, we become impatient and we want to get on with it. We want to know now what it is, because, "I actually want to get on with it." But these things take time. Although I think we have a chosen path, the creation of that path and how it's created is up to us. It's up to us, as individuals, to have the courage to make the choices we need to make, that enable it to happen.

CHAPTER TWELVE

Sometimes we need people to help us. Sometimes we need spiritual teachers or friends or family to say certain things and do certain things to help trigger a response in us that puts us back on our path. Even if it is all unconscious, it is no less divinely inspired. I believe it's all part of our uniqueness, because I believe that if God wanted us to all be the same then I'm pretty sure that God could have figured out how to make us all the same. I think that we need to embrace our uniqueness.

We need to look deeply into our unique situation, our life, and figure out what has happened in our Life Experience that is fundamental to who we are now - and what that could possibly mean for us in finding our purpose. We need to find within our past what it is that is so unique, and use that, adapt that, and embrace that uniqueness to try and see how we can help others, how we can serve humanity, how we can help our friends and family become successful, and how we can help other people connect with what their true purpose is. I believe that for every single one us the purpose is so unique, and so specific to who we are, that nobody else can deliver that particular role.

But if nobody else can deliver that role, and you fail to deliver that role, there's no judgement from the Universe, because the Universe knows the complexities and difficulties of the task at hand.

ENDING YOUR UNCONSCIOUSNESS

It's like a chess game. A chess game can't be won without a whole series of moves. Now, we're not talking about one or two people formulating a strategy here. We're talking millions and billions of people, interacting on a daily basis, all creating slight changes in the overall scheme of things - some of them major, some of them seemingly insignificant, but each of them just as important as the other.

I believe your uniqueness and your purpose on this Earth are directly related. And I think when you start to embrace that, and accept who you are, and Love who you are, the opportunity provided by the Universe starts to be delivered thick and fast. That's certainly been my experience, and it's certainly been the experience of a lot of people that I've worked with. I'm always happy to help you work towards trying to figure out what your purpose in life is.

Think about it. Evaluate yourself. Look into yourself. Embrace yourself. Love yourself. There is a reason why you are here.

That purpose may not be clear to you now, but it's very possible that it will be clear to you soon.

Chapter Thirteen

From Unconscious to Awakening

I know that is a lot to take on board. Some words will have sat well with you, while others would have been more challenging. This is the point. I am trying to challenge you, shake you out of your pre-formed misunderstanding of how life and the Universe operates. Don't worry - it is both normal and expected that you may feel either confused or invigorated, or possibly even both. That is exactly how I felt when I was struck by the lightning bolt of understanding.

Waking up to the fact that you were unconscious to everything going on around you is just the beginning of the overall process. It is the first light of the spring dawn. Although you are not yet consciously aware of it, this is the point you will

ENDING YOUR UNCONSCIOUSNESS

associate to where your awakening has started. Usually we walk around only seeing things as they were, and only from our particular perspective. Like the horse with the blinkers on, we only able to see a certain viewpoint. The awakening that you are embarking on is like seeing everything as it is, when it is, and seeing it from the perspective of all that is around you. It is a beautiful, magical moment when that infinite connection to that One Connected Soul becomes a conscious choice, and not just a mere story.

Seeing things through the eyes of others opens up possibilities that are not only new to you, but also infinite in their possibility. We start to open up new channels, new connections and new beliefs that enable further opportunity. We start seeing synchronicities for why they are happening, as and when they are happening, and no longer well after the fact when the opportunity has already passed. Perspective is everything to the opportunity to open ourselves up enough to see things for what they truly are. It is also confronting, to see for the first time, the range of lies that live in our everyday existence.

However, the process has begun for you now, and so it shall be. We must explore further the realms of the Universe and how you interact with it. We need to talk about your energy, it's immersion with all other energies, and how they will all interact

CHAPTER THIRTEEN

together as a collective singular source. We need to better understand the concepts of vibrational frequency and how to amplify your signal to the Universe of what you desire your life to be.

I am so glad you have chosen to embark on this journey of our soul. Great beings within the Universe are waiting, in timeless space, for you to awaken to your full potential and for you to put theory into action, and prove to yourself of the results that can be had with conscious connected choice. I can share with you what I know, sit with you and explore as much as our lives will allow. I will gladly sit with you, through season after season, for as long as it takes. We will explore and implement what is truly needed for you to not only accept, in your heart of hearts, why you are here and what you came here to do, but also, to have you believe, in the very foundation of all your core beliefs, the words that are setting you free.

I have never expected you to just accept my words wholesale as your own truth, nor do I bear any judgement if you choose to find truth through other means. All I seek is for you to explore the inner workings of your true self, and your place in all this madness. Remember we create our own Life Experience, and it is only created through the thoughts and feelings we have constructed to form it. It is up to you to decide from what - from

ENDING YOUR UNCONSCIOUSNESS

Love or from Fear - but certainly from conscious connected choice.

It's up to you whether it is through unconscious or conscious choice, not me. Nor anyone else for that matter, only you, because the Universe only reflects your thoughts, feelings and actions back to you. I can only guide you, help you and answer the questions you ask. I seek to serve your journey, and help in any way I can, but the work is, and must be, only yours.

I appreciate that looking at your core beliefs is most challenging, but I assure you, that you will soon see it as most liberating. When we fully grasp the simple fact that we have a choice about what beliefs we have and don't have, we can start to understand that the simple act of making the choice sets the path one way or another. You see now that you have complete control over your choices, and you can make whatever choice you want. You can base it on whatever belief you want because beliefs are also a choice.

I am so proud of you for having the courage to come and sit with me on that fateful day on the beach. That takes guts, but again, it is good example of a simple choice that has changed your life forever. There is no turning back now, because I know your thirst for knowledge and abundance in your life has only grown bigger by the thoughts and possibilities of what's ahead.

CHAPTER THIRTEEN

That is a good thing. Let it happen and rejoice in the results of what is yet to come.

Please know: I am not here to be your Hero. I don't want to be. Because the Hero in your story is here to set you free, to positively impact the lives of your friends, and family, your children and the lovers you share yourself with. There is only one true Hero in your story, and that Hero is You.

This journey has only just begun, and it is a tremendous adventure, filled with great challenges, immense secrets and abundant success. It is a journey that only you can travel, a path only you can walk. But have no fear, for I am here always, by your side to guide you towards the best version of yourself that you can possibly create. From here, life may get a little weird, but it will always be entertaining if you so choose it to be. You are never alone, as I will always have your hand.

Now you must be tired. It has been a busy time for us both, and I look forward to us catching up again soon. We have much ground to cover and I am sure you are keen to know more. A good night's sleep always helps us absorb what we have learned and experienced.

Our next discussion is to delve into the secrets of the Universe to expand your consciousness further for your Awakening to Your Truth.

ENDING YOUR UNCONSCIOUSNESS

You not only deserve to know more, but your heart and soul demands it.

That is for good reason, and one you are about to understand.

About the Author

ANDREW HACKETT has more than 20 years of experience helping people think outside their limitations and move beyond their fears so they can accomplish amazing things in their life, business, and relationships.

Connect with Andrew:
https://AndrewHackett.com.au

www.ingramcontent.com/pod-product-compliance
Lightning Source LLC
Chambersburg PA
CBHW051402290426
44108CB00015B/2120